Training Thoroughbred Horses

Preston M. Burch

with the assistance of
Alex Bower

ECHO POINT BOOKS & MEDIA, LLC

Published by Echo Point Books & Media
Brattleboro, Vermont
www.EchoPointBooks.com

ISBN: 978-1-62654-037-8

Cover design by Adrienne Núñez,
Echo Point Books & Media

Editorial and proofreading assistance by Christine Schultz,
Echo Point Books & Media

FOREWORD

If some one little thing in this book helps a young trainer in some way I will feel fully repaid for the time and work that I have put in with Mr. Bower in getting these facts together. I have always considered my father a great horseman and a great trainer of horses and I have tried in a small way to emulate him. He is said to have had more friends on the race track than any man who ever trained horses. Racing has been my whole life, and like my father I love my horses. I felt myself greatly honored when approached by *The Blood-Horse* to write this book.

PRESTON M. BURCH

Table of contents

Preston Burch

(Photo courtesy of Jim Raftery)

THE AUTHOR

Nothing will make a man learn a business faster than to have his own money invested in it. When Preston M. Burch was 18 years old he bought his first Thoroughbred, and he perforce began to train horses to win races. This was in 1902. During the intervening half-century he has been a foremost trainer both in the United States and Europe. He has trained for some of the leading owners in this country, and at present he is the trainer of Mrs. Isabel Dodge Sloane's Brookmeade Stable, whose horses led the American Turf in earnings in 1950 with $651,399 gained from 100 firsts, 94 Seconds, and 61 thirds.

Preston Burch was born in Augusta, Georgia, on August 25, 1881. He was a son of William Preston Burch, who as a boy trained and rode Quarter Horses and served as a courier for General Wade Hampton during the Civil War. William Burch afterward devoted his life to training and met with considerable success at it. Under the tutelage of his father and his uncle, Green B. Morris, one of the great old-time horsemen, Preston Burch learned the sound principles of horsemanship that he has built his own success upon.

In 1902 Preston Burch bought his first horse, a bay gelding named Stuyve, by Stuyvesant - Katie A. by Hyder Ali. The horse won under the Burch colors - blue, orange cuffs, orange cap - a few days after he was bought, and he continued to win under Mr. Burch's training. One of the young horseman's first forays with a public stable was into Canada, where the life of a trainer was real and earnest. He did well up there with the horses of F. R. Hitchcock, John E. Madden, Newton Bennington, H. K. Knapp, and others. In 1905, after another period with his father's stable, he became trainer for the Chelsea Stable owned by Russell Tucker and Ernest La Montagne. On November 7, 1908, he saddled four winners for the Chelsea Stable at Pimlico. They were Taboo, Connaught Ranger, Aster d'Or, and The Wrestler.

In the fall of 1910, after the "Hughes Law" had killed racing in New York, Preston Burch went to France as trainer for Harry La Montagne. While there he also trained for George P. Eustis, William Astor Chanler, and John Sanford. He raced in France, Italy,

Germany, Switzerland, and Belgium, and had success with steeplechasers as well as flat racers. With Harry La Montagne's Sultan VII he won the Grand Steeplechase International, at Milan, Italy's most important steeplechase. After the out-break of World War I he served at the front in France as a volunteer ambulance driver. Later he returned to the States and continued his association with Mr. Sanford. After that he trained George Wingfield's successful Nevada Stock Farm stable for eight years, then trained for Charles T. Fisher. When Mr. Fisher decided to race exclusively in the Middle West, Mr. Burch opened a public stable in the East. Among his patrons were Admiral Cary T. Grayson, Samuel Ross, Mr. and Mrs. Walter M. Jeffords, William du Pont, Mrs. Marion du Pont Scott, and Donald P. Ross. Eventually he gave up the public stable to train for Mr. and Mrs. Jeffords. Later he reopened a public stable and trained for Harry La Montagne, Henry Lustig, and Richard and Deering Howe.

In 1943 he assumed the management of Mrs. Sloane's breeding and racing establishments. As in training horses, he had gained his early experience as a breeder through putting up his own money. The first stakes winner bred by him was Spic and Span, a daughter of Whisk Broom II - Sub Rosa, by Disguise. With one of his broodmare purchases he struck an unexpected lode: he bought the mare Castanet, by *Frizzle - Kaskaskia by Yankee, which was supposed to be barren at the time but had been bred to Fair Play. The next spring she delivered a foal which Mr. Burch sold at a profit. Later he bred her to General Thatcher, one of his favorites among the horses he had trained, and from the mating obtained a filly. He had been selling Castanet's produce, but on the advice of Thomas Carr Piatt he kept the General Thatcher filly. She developed into Tambour, which Mr. Burch sent out to win the Selima Stakes, the Coaching Club American Oaks, and more than $75,000. He owned the broodmare Gallette, and in partnership with his friend W. L. Brann, bred from her Gallorette, one of our greatest race mares.

Mr. Burch's eye for young racing prospects led him to select George Smith, the 1916 Kentucky Derby winner, for John Sanford. He later trained the horse as a 5-year-old, when he was considered the best handicapper of the year, and had the pleasure of seeing him win the Bowie Handicap over *Omar Khayyam and Exterminator, two other Derby winners.

Among other good horses trained by Mr. Burch have been Firethorn, winner of the Lawrence Realization, the Suburban Handicap, and the Jockey Club Gold Cup (twice); Boatswain, winner of the Withers Stakes; Regal Lily, an Alabama winner; Creole Maid, a Coaching Club American Oaks winner; Wand, winner of the Matron Stakes; Sweep All, winner of the Endurance Handicap; *White Clover, winner of the Suburban Handicap; the great steeple-chaser Battleship; True North, winner of the Fall Highweight Handicap under 140 pounds; and many others. The Brookmeade Stable horses of 1950, when the stable led the money-winning list, included the stakes winners Greek Ship, Sunglow, Atalanta, Going Away, Dart By, and Ouija. The stable also included the 2-year-old Bold, which won the Preakness Stakes the following year. The 1952 stable included Sky Ship, winner of the Florida Derby, and Tritium, winner of the Selima Stakes.

As evidence of the regard in which he is held by other trainers, Preston Burch, one of the founders of the American Trainers Association, was elected the first president, and held the office seven years.

Besides developing good horses, Mr. Burch has had a hand in educating some first-class trainers. These include Richard Handlen, Burley Parke (who was under him as an apprentice jockey and later as stable agent and assistant trainer), and Oscar White. The most recent of his "students" is his son Elliott Burch, who assists with the Brookmeade Stable and has the family love for horses. The late Selby Burch, a brother to Preston Burch, also was prominent as a trainer.

Horses trained by Preston Burch have won in Europe, Canada, Mexico, Cuba, and all parts of the United States - Illinois, Florida, California, Louisiana, Kentucky, Ohio, Michigan, Maryland, West Virginia, New York, New Jersey, Rhode Island, Massachusetts.

He is generous with advice and help for younger trainers, and he will usually find an opportunity to tell them: "Make winning a purse your first objective. Make betting incidental."

. . . yearlings must have proper exercise if they are to make good racehorses.
(Photo courtesy of Suzie Oldham)

Selection of Racing Material

IT SHOULD BE UNDERSTOOD at the outset that there are no hard and fast rules for the selection of young horses to be used for racing. There are certain considerations that may be used as guides for selection, but they are only general principles and it will not be unusual to encounter exceptions to them.

In selecting yearlings as prospective race horses, a trainer considers some basic points. For example he would avoid choosing a yearling with too-straight pasterns, a narrow head, small eyes, a shoulder that does not set properly, sickle hocks, feet that toe in or out, small or contracted feet, and narrow hips. Neither would he want a yearling with a dull or listless personality, indicating a lack of spirit and animation and giving the impression of the absence of intelligence and responsiveness.

A well-set pastern is sloped at an angle of about 45 degrees from the cannon bone, which is the portion of the leg between the ankle and the knee or the hock. If the pastern seems to stem directly from the cannon bone, it is too straight. Such a pastern places an undue strain on some tendons and ligaments, and the horse may be expected to go lame eventually. The lameness may show up in the ankle joint or the knee; more likely it will be in the knee. When a horse is galloping, each leg in turn supports his entire weight and if the pastern is too straight the ankle joint does not flex enough to absorb its share of the impact. The shock from galloping therefore is transmitted to the upper part of the leg, especially the knee.

A short pastern is much preferred to one that is too long, although a pastern can be too short, giving a horse a pony-like construction. On the other hand, a pastern that is too long tends to over strain the tendons. I also have seen horses with long pasterns cut their elbows while galloping, when the fore leg was folded back at the end of a stride, because of the unusual length of pastern. A young horseman would bet that that couldn't happen. I would have doubted

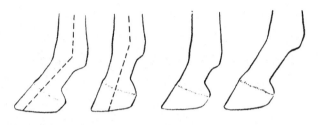

NORMAL PASTERN   STRAIGHT   SHORT   LONG
45 °   PASTERN   PASTERN   PASTERN

When a horse is galloping, each leg in turn supports his entire weight.
(*Photo Courtesy of Thoroughbred Publications, Inc.*)

it too, until I saw it. One horse that I trained cut his elbows so badly because of long pasterns that I had to race him without shoes on his front feet. In fact I have trained two horses that hit their elbows this way, and many older horsemen have had the same experience.

Horses with shoulders that are set on too straight do not, as a rule, run very far. When a shoulder is set too close to the vertical the horse is not well equipped mechanically for striding out and getting over the ground. His reach is limited. He has to work harder than a horse with a well-set shoulder, and he tires more easily. Nine out of ten good horses - the percentage may be even higher - have a nice sloping shoulder.

NORMAL SHOULDER   STRAIGHT SHOULDER

Sickle hocks are ugly, but I am not certain just how much of a handicap they are. Mechanically they seem to be all wrong, because they limit the extension of the hind leg and would not seem to be adapted for long, easy strides. It also seems likely that they are a sufficient departure from normal to place a strain on other parts of a horse's running machinery. However, some good race horses have had sickle hocks, and possibly a young horse should not be faulted too much if his hind legs are not quite straight. It probably is a good idea, though, to reject a horse whose hocks are out of line to an exaggerated degree.

The two best horses I ever trained were George Smith and General Thatcher. Both had perfectly straight hocks. But Tambour and Voltear, two other good horses that I trained, had very bad hock action when they were running. Tambour, whom I bred, won the Selima Stakes and the Coaching Club American Oaks, among other races. Her hindlegs twisted so badly when she was running that I had to put clamps on her rear plates so she wouldn't twist them off. Voltear, winner of the Chesapeake Stakes and other good races, had similar trouble.

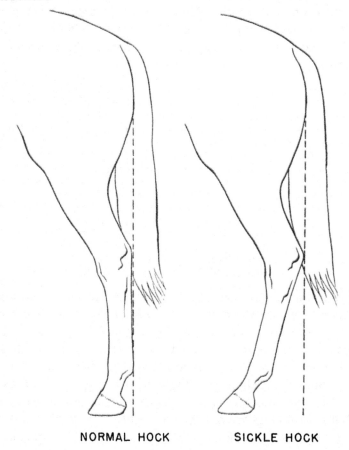

NORMAL HOCK   SICKLE HOCK

I don't like a horse whose hocks are set too close together, like a cow's. They do not have smooth action, and they generally interfere. A horse who interferes hits his legs together, causing cuts and bruises. Improper shoeing will often throw a horse off balance and cause him to cut himself. If a horse is perfectly made, a good blacksmith can stop him from hitting himself, but if the hocks are malformed or the feet and legs are not set properly, the blacksmith can't do much about it.

A horse with a cannon bone that is "tied-in" is more likely to go wrong than a horse with wide bone. A tied-in cannon bone is narrower than it should be just below the back of the knee. The tendons of the lower leg therefore are out of line and are subjected to abnormal strain. And of course the narrowing of the bone means that the bone structure at that point is not as strong as it should be.

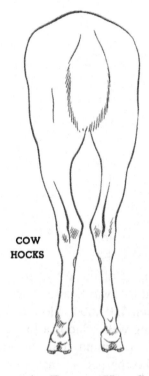

COW HOCKS

I thoroughly dislike calf-kneed horses, or horses "back at the knee." They invariably go wrong in the tendon just behind the knee, and they invariably go wrong early. A case that brings this strongly to mind concerns some of the produce of the broodmare Flota, owned by Brookmeade Farm. Her first foal, Warship, was calf-kneed. He went wrong very early in his 2-year-old season. He was turned out for a year and was brought back to the races in 1946, as a 3-year-old. He went wrong again in a winning race and didn't start again until 1948. He won in 1948 and 1949. He was a grand looking horse except for being calf-kneed, and I am sure that he was cut out to be a top racer. Flota's second foal was Airmada. He had the same calf knees. He went wrong early in his 2-year-old training and was turned out on the farm. He was not sound enough to stand training until 1948, when he won as a 4-year-old. After a rest at the farm he came back again to win in 1950, when he was six years old. He was not as good looking as Warship and was not as good a horse, but he would have been a most useful animal had it not been for his knees.

17

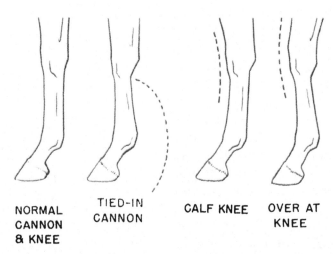

NORMAL CANNON & KNEE   TIED-IN CANNON   CALF KNEE   OVER AT KNEE

Because of these two foals, we all but sold the mare. However, her third foal was Seaward, whose knees are normal and who has won more than $200,000. Flota still is owned by Brookmeade Farm and is producing well. She is a handsome, well made mare and there is no doubt in my mind that the faulty knees of Warship and Airmada cannot be charged against her.

A horse that is "over" at the knees, which is the opposite of calf knees, generally trains all right, though his knees are a bit ugly. This condition usually becomes more pronounced as a horse grows older, and some people might object to it in a stallion because of its unsightliness. However, I am sure that it doesn't bother the horse.

A horse that toes in or out is very likely to strike himself while running, and again such a variation from what we call the normal places an abnormal strain on other parts of the leg. This strain may fall on the ankles, or if the twist in the leg structure that causes a horse to toe in or out originates near the knee, then it may be expected that if trouble develops, it will be in the knee.

Horses that are forked wide in front, with too much space between the legs where they come out of the chest, should not be expected to run a distance. It is hard to give a reason for this, but apparently a wide-forked horse has some lost motion when he runs, and he tends to tire more easily than other horses.

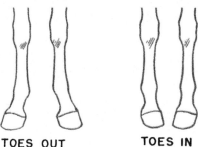

TOES OUT   TOES IN

A horse with a narrow head is likely to have less intelligence than a horse with good width between his eyes. This may be a simple matter of how much room he has in his skull for brains. Intelligence goes with good horses. If a horse is intelligent, he shows it in his general expression and bearing. Many horse-men, when examining a young racing prospect, pause a short distance from him and take in his overall appearance, paying particular attention to whether he impresses them as being alert and interested in what is going on around him. If they like his personality, they proceed to a more detailed inspection.

Horses with narrow feet tend to go sore, especially over hard race tracks. Since narrow feet provide a small weightbearing surface, the impact from running often causes such feet to spread at the quarters, and sometimes a broken bone results. I have also seen a great many horses with narrow feet develop tendon trouble at the back of and under the knee.

The frog is an important part of a horse's foot. It is spongy, like a rubber cushion, and it really is the cushion of the foot. The foot receives the greatest shock when a horse is running. Nature made the spongy frog to absorb the first terrific shock of a thousand-pound horse galloping over a hard surface at high speed. The more frog in the foot, the more cushion a horse lands on when he is running. A narrow foot is inclined to become even more narrow and contracted unless it is cared for by an expert. The more a foot contracts, the smaller the frog becomes and the more difficult it is to get adequate frog pressure. A horse with narrow, contracted feet lands on the outer walls of the heels and must eventually go lame. The normal expansion and contraction of the frog keeps a foot healthy and sound.

A contracted foot with inadequate frog does not get sufficient blood circulation.

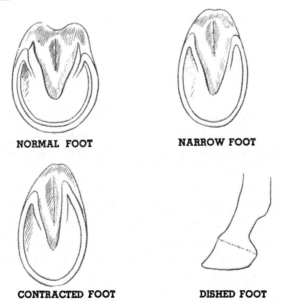

NORMAL FOOT   NARROW FOOT

CONTRACTED FOOT   DISHED FOOT

I have heard buyers criticized for picking up and examining the foot of a sales yearling while the horse was being shown in public. The criticism was expressed by breeders who thought onlookers might get the impression that there was something wrong with the yearling's feet. I do not think that breeders should resent this, because a buyer certainly ought to examine the feet of a horse he is interested in. But maybe the better way is to wait until the horse is taken back into his stall. The feet then can be examined in private and with less danger that the buyer will be kicked if the yearling is excitable.

A yearling with either a ringbone or a dished foot is a poor risk. Dished feet generally are caused in a dry season by the contraction of the hoof from lack of moisture. Horses with dished feet are more likely to go wrong than horses with good feet. A dished foot may also be a congenital deformity or it may indicate that an inflammatory condition has been present. Ringbone may cause lameness either because of the irritation it causes within the foot or through mechanical interference with the movement of a joint.

A horse with narrow hips cannot be as strong and muscular as one with wide hips. A man with broad shoulders and substantial hips is very likely to be a better athlete than a narrow-chested fellow. I think the same holds true with broad-hipped horses.

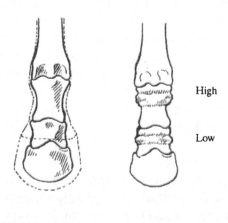

High

Low

NORMAL FOOT   RINGBONE

I like a yearling with a swinging walk. If a horse walks sloppily it is likely that he will be sloppy in other ways. I like to see one that reaches out with a good stride in his hind legs. Some of the old-time horsemen considered it a good sign if a horse overstrode with his hind legs. They would examine the ground to see if the marks left by his hind feet extended beyond the prints of his front feet.

A horse with a short neck lacks balance. This type of horse tends to tire when attempting to run a distance, possibly because his lack of balance causes him to expend more energy. Ewe-necked horses are ugly, like horses with Roman noses, but a ewe neck or a Roman nose doesn't affect a horse's running ability.

A swaybacked horse is homely to look at, but a sway back seems to be as strong as a normal back. The great swayback of all times was Tenny, one of the best horses ever seen in America. An old horse who used to race in the West was named Sway, because of his back. He looked as if he were made in two parts, but he could run. I wouldn't buy a sway-backed horse, but if I had one, his back wouldn't stop me from training him.

A goose-rumped horse, like a swaybacked horse is not pretty to look at, but it is a fault that can be disregarded, just as you might accept a leggy horse if he has compensating good points. It is difficult to find a perfect horse. Sometimes you see a horse who is almost perfect physically, but he can't run much. Knowing this, we must be prepared to accept some little defects if a horse pleases us otherwise.

In selecting yearlings one must remember that a horse perfect in every way can grow out of shape and develop an unsoundness. On the other hand, a horse may improve enough in regard to some slight defect that it will be scarcely noticeable in a year's time. Sometimes a knowledge of a yearling's sire or dam may be a guide to a buyer. For example, if a buyer knows that the dam had a defect in conformation but was a good race mare, he may be inclined to overlook a similar defect in one of her foals.

I like short cannon bones. A short cannon, like a short pastern, means a longer upper leg and consequently a longer stride. I also like a good depth of chest. I don't like pony-built horses.

A horse should have a good width of bone, and the tendons should be clearly defined. There should be no puffy ankle joints. The desirability of wide, flat bones was mentioned in connection with tieing-in.

A yearling with splints or bog spavins is very likely to be soft-boned, with a predisposition to unsoundness. Possibly he has been

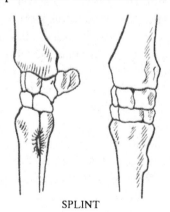

SPLINT

Side view   Front View

overfed or under exercised. A splint on the cannon bone, or shin bone, is not too serious if it doesn't interfere with a tendon. It probably will not bother the horse. But it must be remembered that a horse with one splint will generally develop more of them. A splint that is pressing against a tendon is sure to cause trouble.

When inspecting a horse for possible purchase one should examine his throat and jaw to see if he has plenty of room for his windpipe. My father never failed to insert his fist where the jaw comes out of the neck, at the throatlatch. If there was plenty of room for his fist, he felt that there was ample room for the horse's windpipe. If the space was too narrow for the fist, he believed that the horse would have difficulty in breathing when in a race. For the same reason he always examined a horse's nostrils, to make certain that they were large enough to permit the horse to inhale and exhale easily when running.

When I look at a sales yearling I always consider the record of the farm he comes from. I like to buy from a farm whose horses have scored some recent successes. That shows me that the horses have been properly cared for and the breeder knows what he is doing, and that the farm has good soil.

My advice to a trainer who buys fat sales yearlings is to turn them out on grass immediately after the sale and feed them little but grass for from four to six weeks. Most sales yearlings are too fat for their own good, and the excess weight has to be taken off them before they can be broken without risk of damage or injury. A great many yearlings that are fat and soft are also soft-boned. They develop infirmities as a result of too much feed and too much weight and not enough exercise for would-be athletes.

In defense of market breeders who offer fat sales yearlings, I must admit that they are on a spot. Trainers constantly complain about fat yearlings, but they are suspicious of thin ones. A thin yearling doesn't get a second look, because a trainer immediately suspects that he is a poor doer, which he doesn't want in his stable, or that he has been through a recent sickness, or that he is from a poorly managed farm, or that he has been neglected.

I do believe, however, that there should he a happy medium for sales yearlings. Market breeders realize that a sales yearling has to be in top condition to bring a top price. But they also know that yearlings must have proper exercise if they are to make good race horses. I have seen yearlings so fat that I wouldn't bid on them, though I liked them otherwise. Some of them turned out well in spite of the fat. When inspecting sales yearlings, I look for ones in sound physical condition and in medium flesh, not hog fat.

In the days of good old Sheepshead Bay, when yearlings were sometimes brought to the sales as early as June, they were broken immediately after their purchase, with no apparent ill effects. They were nothing like as fat as they are nowadays. At that time yearlings were not as well grown as they are now, and there was no such thing as a too-fat yearling. They were handled very little on the farms, were never pampered, and consequently they were hard to break, but some mighty tough horses were turned out in those days.

Breaking Yearlings

AT BROOKMEADE FARM, the breaking of the home-bred yearlings is started in late June or early July. Any yearlings we buy at the sales are turned out for from four to six weeks, as mentioned previously, and are broken later, along in September and October.

As the first step in acquainting a young racing prospect with his new role in life, I suggest that he be made accustomed to the bridle. The bridle should be put on over the halter. The halter is always used under the bridle until a yearling is well broken, because a halter is stronger in case a yearling has to be restrained with a shank during the breaking procedure. If a shank is used on a bridle, it will cause the bit to hurt the horse's mouth. When the bridle is first put on a yearling, it should be done most carefully, because an unhappy experience at this time can make a horse head-shy. The person who puts the bridle on a yearling should be careful not to pinch his ears or frighten him.

If a yearling shows the slightest sign of being frightened or uneasy when being bridled, I recommend that the bridle be taken apart. Put the head-piece carefully over his ears, then slip the bit gently into his mouth and buckle the cheekpieces onto the headpiece. If the bridle is not unbuckled in this fashion, the bit must be put into the yearling's mouth first, and the headpiece more or less forced over his ears. But by unbuckling the bridle and putting the pieces on separately, the groom or handler can avoid a tussle with a yearling at a stage when a young horse is suspicious and impressionable.

The cheekpiece should be adjusted so the bit is fairly tight in the mouth. If the bridle is put on loosely and the bit hangs in the yearling's mouth, he will play with the bit and eventually get his tongue over it. This can develop into a bad habit. It makes a horse difficult to control. Many horses race with their tongue tied down so they can't get it over the bit. This habit is usually acquired in the early stages of bitting.

The bridle should always be put on over the halter . . . If a yearling shows the slightest sign of being frightened or uneasy when being bridled . . . the bridle should be taken apart. Put the headpiece carefully over his ears . . .

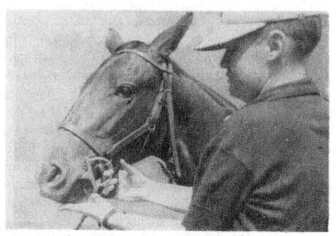

. . . then slip the bit gently into his mouth . . .

The importance of gentle handling when the bridle is first put on a yearling cannot be overstressed. A horse's ears are sensitive. This could be especially true if they have been abscessed or injured at some time prior to breaking. Head-shyness is an exasperating trait in a horse, and is difficult to overcome. Rough or awkward movements in this stage of a yearling's education may upset him for months. Gentleness at this time is well repaid in the future.

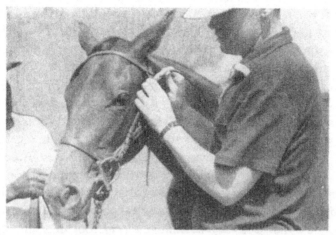

. . . and buckle the cheekpieces onto the headpiece . . .

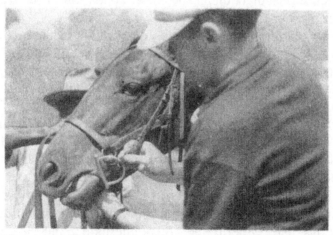

The cheekpieces should be adjusted so the bit is fairly tight in the mouth.

Everyone connected with the breaking and handling of yearlings should be slow and deliberate in his movements. A quick movement of the body or a sudden gesture with the hand will often frighten a young horse, with bad results. The only excusable quick move is in getting away from a yearling's teeth or heels.

When a yearling has become thoroughly accustomed to the bridle and allows you to put it on and take it off without any trouble, he can advance to the next phase of breaking. This consists of getting him used to a surcingle, with a pommel pad or saddle pad on his withers. The surcingle is put on gently and tightened gradually. The yearling then is got used to moving around the stall, turning in all directions, while wearing bridle and surcingle. After he has learned this he can be taken out of the stall and led around for a while. When he gets so that he pays no attention to the pad and surcingle, a saddle can be put on him, with the stirrups removed. Dangling stirrups often slap a horse's flanks and frighten him. Sometimes it happens, too, that a horse will toss his head around to swipe at a fly or at an itchy spot caused by the girth and will get his jaw caught in the stirrup. It also has happened that a horse has caught a rear foot in a stirrup when striking at a fly or trying to scratch an itchy spot.

All moves in the early education of yearlings should be performed by experienced handlers under the close supervision of the trainer or one of his assistants.

When a yearling remains perfectly quiet with a saddle on his back, put him in a stall and get a boy on him. Sometimes this will be approached gradually. For instance, the boy may not sit on the yearling's back at once, but may hang over the saddle on his stomach, getting the yearling used to the feel of weight on his back. The boy will pat him on the sides and flanks to calm him and assure him that nothing terrible is happening. When this method is used, the boy, with assistance from someone holding the yearling's head, eases into the saddle after the yearling is accustomed to the weight and doesn't seem to be frightened by it.

Some trainers prefer to put a boy up with a saddle pad instead of a saddle at this time. Other trainers do not hesitate to put the saddle on immediately after the bridle, not resorting to the more careful way of giving a yearling a lesson with surcingle and pad first. The latter is the slower, surer way. To my mind it is advisable, though perhaps not always necessary, even with a yearling that has been handled considerably at the farm.

This part of the schooling is always done in the stall. There is less room for a yearling to jump around when he is in a stall, and less likelihood that he or the boy will get hurt. If a yearling seems skittish, it is a good idea to place a man on each side of him. In one hand each man will hold a shank attached to the halter, with the other hand free to hold the boy by the leg, if necessary. This gives good control over the yearling and helps the boy retain his balance and stay on in the event of a rumpus. It should be impressed on the boy that it is very important for him not to be thrown. If a yearling makes a couple of jumps and doesn't throw the boy, your troubles may be over. A trainer is fortunate if he can get through these preliminary stages without having a boy thrown, because if a young horse finds out that he can dump a boy, he will delight in repeating it again and again.

The men holding the shanks should be competent and agile and should use gentleness and persuasion instead of loud talk and swearing. They are not likely to be hurt if they stay close to the yearling's shoulder and don't get in front of him where he can run over them or strike them with a foot.

After a yearling is used to the weight of a boy on his back, and can be led and turned in all directions, he can be taken out of the stall. With some yearlings the procedure from bridling to carrying a boy may take several days. Others learn more quickly. It is important that the handlers call it a day when a yearling shows signs of becoming tired and hot. Stop before the yearling begins to fight. Resume the lesson the next day.

Yearlings of the present, accustomed to being handled from the time they are foaled, usually adapt themselves very well to the routine of breaking. It is not exceptional for a yearling to accept the bridle and the boy in one session, with only one man helping. It has been my experience that if you are quiet and gentle with them, yearlings can be broken quickly and easily. In recent years it has not been uncommon for us to start from scratch and put boys on half a dozen yearlings during a single morning.

Once in a while a trainer comes across a yearling that gives trouble. In France one time I had a big rough colt who would be going along as if he had learned his lessons. Then suddenly he would slump to the ground and try to roll over on the boy. This went on for

29

a while, and I made up my mind to do something about it. I told my stable foreman, a big fellow, to sit on the colt's head the next time he tried that trick. The foreman did this, pinning the colt to the ground while I worked him over with a whip. That cured him. I didn't like to use such drastic treatment, but he had given so much trouble that it was the only thing to do.

When a yearling gets so that he pays no attention to the saddle pad and surcingle . . .

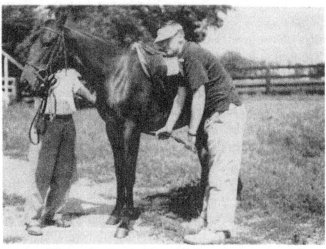

. . . a saddle can be put on him with the stirrups removed . . .

After a yearling is used to the bridle and doesn't mind having a boy on his back, it is time to get him out on the walking ring in company with some of the other yearlings. There are a varying number of yearlings in a set. A trainer with a dozen yearlings, for example, may take them out in two sets of six or three sets of four, depending on how many exercise boys he has available. The first lessons on the outdoor walking ring consist of merely walking the yearlings around the circle, getting them further accustomed to the bridles and the boys. It is well to have a quiet lead pony in front of them, rather than trying to make a leader out of one of the yearlings. Horses will follow a leader, and a quiet pony helps keep the yearlings calm. During the early part of this phase of their education, each yearling will be accompanied by a groom, who will lead him with a shank. As soon as the yearlings are used to following the pony the grooms can turn them loose and walk beside them until they are assured that they will move along quietly.

Walking on the ring may be continued until the yearlings are following in good style. Then they can be stepped up to a trot. During their first lessons in walking and trotting they should always circle to the left. When they become tractable they should be circled to the right, part of the time. When they get so they trot easily around the circle in either direction, they should be moved to a larger area where they can trot in a figure eight. This quickly makes them bridle-wise. The pony still accompanies them in this exercise.

When the yearlings are jogging well, they can be stepped up to a slow canter. All this will take some few days. The yearlings will go a little farther and do a little more as they become fit and well behaved. At this point they still haven't been on the race track. When they have mastered their lessons this far the pony can be dispensed with and the yearlings can take turns leading the set. But if this causes too much commotion it is better to resume with the pony and wait a while before trying the yearlings by themselves again.

Yearlings should never be sent onto the race track where other horses are training until they are absolutely bridle-wise. If you try to hurry them onto the track before they know what the bridle is for, they are hard to control and can easily hurt themselves or another horse, or injure a boy.

When they have mastered their lessons . . .
(Photo Courtesy of Suzie Oldham)

. . . the yearlings can take turns leading the set.
(Photo courtesy of Louise Reinegel)

When the race track phase of their schooling has begun, yearlings should get a lot of slow work at first. They should be walked slowly, cantered slowly, and galloped slowly. It is good for them to learn to go single file, and two abreast, and three or more abreast if you have room enough on the track and are working enough yearlings in a set. All of them should have turns on the inside of the set, on the outside, in the lead, and following.

Yearlings should be taught to stand quietly in a line on the track. They should learn to walk abreast in any direction, to stop and stand quietly, and to back up. Most of them readily learn to back up when the boy tightens the reins. If one of them is a little stubborn about backing up, he will learn his lesson if you tap him gently on the shins with a light cane or a switch. Learning to back up is important for race horses. The situation often arises in the starting gate when it is necessary for them to take a step backward if they are too close to the doors.

Yearlings should never be sent onto the race track where other horses are training until they are absolutely bridlewise.
(Photo Courtesy of Suzie Oldham)

Race horses are so accustomed to working to the left, because of the counter-clockwise training and racing in the United States, that it is important to see they do sufficient work to the right, otherwise you will end up with one-rein horses. This is why yearlings should frequently be turned to the right when walking and even cantering, when possible.

The breaking of yearlings requires time and patience and understanding. The trainer and the boys and men handling yearlings at breaking time must understand that shouting at a yearling and fighting with him is the wrong thing to do. Yearlings that are handled gently at breaking time respond to this kindness and usually become gentle horses.

It is good for them to learn to go single file, and two abreast, and three or more abreast.
Photo courtesy of Suzie Oldham

Some trainers have their yearlings broken to harness before they are broken to ride. This is an excellent idea because it accustoms a yearling to the bridle and teaches him to handle himself before weight is put on his back. But the average trainer hasn't the time or facilities for this, and not much of it is done. It really isn't necessary, but it's all right if you want to do it.

This recalls a story about the oft-quoted John E.Madden. At the time Mr. Madden was breaking yearlings it was the custom for horses to be jogged down the track for perhaps three-quarters of a mile before they were sent into a gallop. Mr.Madden showed up with a bunch of horses that jogged off for only two or three paces and started to gallop. "Why don't you trot your horses ?" someone asked. "Because I'm not training trotters," was the reply. In my opinion the present custom of giving a horse just a short jog before breaking into a gallop was adapted from Mr. Madden's innovation.

They should learn to walk abreast in any direction, . . .
(Photo courtesy of Suzie Oldham)

I generally use some green boys on yearlings because I find that it is a good time to teach boys to ride. Someone has to teach them or eventually we would have no exercise boys. After the first few lessons, yearlings generally become quiet enough for the little boys to handle, and the boys can learn while the horses are learning. If this combination is worked properly, the boys learn to ride and the yearlings benefit from the lighter weight.

Trainers in the larger stables receive numerous applications from light-weight boys who want to become riders. In the Brookmeade Stable we sift the applicants carefully and choose a few young boys each year. In selecting a boy who may possibly develop into a race rider, it is well to know that his parents are small in stature. This most likely indicates that the boy will remain light for a long enough time to be useful to the stable as an exercise boy and possibly a jockey. Such a boy should have small bones and small feet, and be strong, healthy, and intelligent, with a real desire to work with horses. Many of our best jockeys have come from the West, where they were brought up on farms and knew and worked with horses from childhood.

. . . to stop and stand quietly, and to back up.
(Photo by Paul Schafer, Courtesy of NYRA)

If in a set of yearlings you find an especially difficult one, he should not be entrusted to one of the new boys. He should be handled by an experienced rider, even if the boy is on the heavy side.

It will not hurt yearlings to carry a bit of weight while they are going slowly. However, if you use a rider weighing more than say 130 pounds, you are inviting an unsoundness in a young horse from carrying too much weight. This is especially true when yearlings begin to do a little fast work. Fast moves, it should be understood, are not to be attempted until the yearlings are ready for them. For example, when you have your yearlings walking, jogging, and cantering for a total of at least 2 1/2 miles each day, and they are doing it without strain or discomfort, you can give them their first lesson at something faster by telling the boys to let them move along for the last eighth or three-sixteenths mile of their gallop.

A breeze is something a bit faster than a fast gallop. The best way to breeze yearlings at first is to put them two abreast. By putting them abreast, they will learn from each other and they go much better when they have company. Later on they can be breezed single file or by twos, close together, one set behind the other, so they learn to get a little dirt in the face. They must be accustomed to this before they race, so they will not duck out or refuse to extend themselves when the dirt hits them. Nothing fast should be attempted until the youngsters are fit enough and until they have had sufficient slow breezing to assure the trainer that they will go in a straight path. They must be changed frequently from inside to outside and from front to rear positions. The boys must be cautioned to keep the yearlings close together, and the boy on the rail must stay as close to it as safety permits. When the yearlings are being eased up after a breeze they should be taken to about the middle of the race track. Allowing them to go to the outside rail when pulling up must be avoided at all times, because horses acquire the runout habit very easily.

Early breezing, starting with about an eighth of a mile, can be carried up to a quarter of a mile. Yearlings are given short, slow breezes at first. The distance and speed are increased as the trainer finds them ready for extended work. The faster moves may be given at intervals of several days, until the yearlings learn to jump away quickly and run fast for a short distance. However, once a yearling learns how to run fast, his fastest moves should be sandwiched in between slow breezes. Yearlings are generally galloped seven days a week. On a farm where they are being turned out constantly they may simply be turned out on Sunday instead of galloped. If they are not being turned out regularly it does not pay to walk them on Sunday in lieu of regular work because they forget their lessons easily. Besides, they may be too fresh on Monday, after a day's rest, and some of the boys are likely to be thrown off.

If one or more of a group of yearlings show undue nervousness or excitement, the speed work of these individuals must be reduced or eliminated until they quiet down. Now and then one finds a yearling who seems to know all about speed right from the start. This fellow should be restrained and not allowed to overdo.

Some of the yearlings will develop bucked shins early in their training. The term "bucked shins" comes from the appearance of the shin when this condition exists. It bucks outward, forming a convex swelling on the front of the shin. The swelling is accompanied by heat, soreness, and extreme pain. A horse that is badly bucked may flinch if you merely point your finger at his shins or move as if you are going to touch them. I think the more frequent occurrence of bucked shins today is caused by softer horses and harder tracks.

When a horse's shins buck it means that he develops an inflammation of the periosteum, or covering of the shin bone. It comes, as a rule, after a few fast moves. Bucking generally occurs first in the left front shin. It may begin with a slight soreness in one or both front shins, or it may become terribly sore from just one good work. A soft, fat horse can develop bucked shins after just a few slow breezes, and sometimes one of these soft fellows will buck in front and behind, in all four shins.

I have seen horses run remarkable races on sore ankles, sore knees, or sore feet, but seldom have I seen a horse run one of his top races on sore shins. The pain from sore shins is something they will not go up against, and for this reason I never ask my horses to do anything when their shins are sore. I think a horse can acquire all sorts of bad habits if forced to do something when he is bucked.

In treating bucked shins one should get the fever and soreness out and put a blister on the shins to toughen them. Antiphlogistine is a good thing to use in case of swelling or soreness on the shins or elsewhere. I have also found that a mixture of clay with a little Epsom salts, glycerine, and vinegar is just about as effective as

Antiphlogistine, and costs less. In applying Antiphlogistine it is a good idea to put it on thick enough to last several days. If there is a lot of fever in the shin, the Antiphlogistine will turn quite hard in a couple of days. When this happens the old dressing should be washed off and a fresh one put on. After Antiphlogistine is applied to the shin, a piece of brown wrapping paper is put over it, and cotton and bandages over that. The brown paper prevents the cotton from soaking up the Antiphlogistine and it assists the sweating process set up by the medication. The clay also can be used with paper and cotton and bandages but it is effective when applied without any covering. If it is not covered, the clay will dry out during the day. A fresh application can be put on over the dry clay. The clay or Antiphlogistine treatment should be continued until all the fever and soreness have been taken out of the shins. Then a blister can be applied. I have no real preferences among blisters, but have had very good luck using a fairly strong blister on shins. Never put a blister on an area that has fever in it because a severe inflammation will result, which sometimes leaves the affected parts enlarged.

Besides bucked shins, one of the first troubles encountered with yearlings is a puffiness around the ankles. If not treated, the puffiness will develop into osselets, which are bony growths occurring around the front part of the ankle. They result from a leakage of fluid from the ankle joint. If the development of osselets is not halted, they continue to grow in size, sometimes enormously, making an ankle look twice its normal size. The growth becomes calcified and frequently causes a stiffness of the ankle joint. Sometimes the movement of the joint becomes entirely impaired. When puffy ankles are first noticed, further trouble may be prevented by the use of a mixture of half alcohol and half glycerine, rubbed into the ankles twice a day while the horse is in his stall. Cotton and bandages are applied after the mixture is rubbed in. If this doesn't work, it may be necessary to use one of the modern ankle paints, supplied by most veterinarians. If the swelling persists, one must stop work with the horse. After the swelling and fever have subsided, have the ankles punch-fired. If a horse is turned out on a farm and rested for from three to six months he will come out with perfectly clean ankles, but he could well develop the same trouble when you train him again. We in America don't often have the time to turn horses out, so we resort to firing, which as a rule prevents a recurrence of this kind of trouble.

The breezing and working of yearlings may continue until the trainer is satisfied with what they have shown. The ones with good action, good manners, and sufficient speed may be considered potential stakes winners. Fast trials at a quarter-mile may be done in 23 to 24 seconds, depending on the speed of the horse and the track over which he is tried. In general, 23 seconds on an average track is considered a very good move for a quarter-mile. In their faster moves the yearlings are usually paired according to ability, putting the quick ones together and keeping the slower ones together. In this way the slower ones do not get discouraged from being beaten continually, and usually they will improve gradually, if they have it in them. It is best not to resort to a whip unless you have a lazy, sluggish horse who simply will not show any speed without it. In the old days, spurs were frequently used on this kind of horse. They are seldom used today, but they can be helpful on stubborn horses.

As a rule fillies learn more quickly than colts. However, they also are more excitable and are generally harder to handle, but now and then you will find a colt who wants to be a real tough hombre.

Several ring bits are a necessary part of the equipment in a training stable. The ring fits over the lower jaw of a horse and brings a slight pressure against the jaw when an animal is inclined to bear in or out. It is not a severe bit and it will not stop a bad runout horse, but it will be a big help in the beginning, when a young horse may be slightly inclined to go to one side instead of straight ahead. It very often prevents such a horse from acquiring the habit of running out or bearing in. A regular snaffle bit is generally used on yearlings. It should not be too long, as yearlings have narrower muzzles than older horses. The bit should not extend outside the mouth.

Sometimes it is effective to put blinkers on slow or lazy yearlings. This is always done with a bit of caution, because a green horse with blinkers on can easily become frightened and injure himself or another horse. A good plan is to put the blinkers on a yearling after his gallop. Put them on while he is walking on the ring, cooling out, or even in his stall after he is put away. A yearling should be cantered in blinkers for a day or more before asking him to go faster than a gallop. He should always have company at this time to allay his fears.

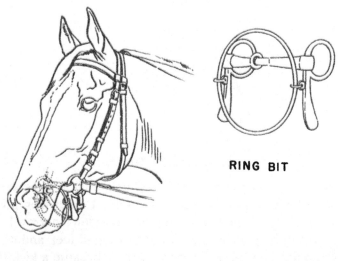

RING BIT

RING BIT

After yearlings have been tried, which has required a training period of two to three months, and the trainer feels satisfied that he can make an estimate of their ability, he gives them a let-up from any speed work, but continues the slow gallops. If he should be on a farm he may decide simply to turn them out in the paddocks for a few weeks. In any case, this period of comparative rest is a good time for horses to receive worm treatments. It is very necessary to test horses for worms from time to time, and treat them when they need it. This is determined by having a veterinarian make a microscopic examination of the droppings for worm eggs. Yearlings that are infested with worms should be treated under the direction of a veterinarian or someone else experienced in giving the treatments.

I keep my yearlings barefooted as long as possible, which is until the foot shows signs of extreme wear or becomes broken in places. When one or another of these conditions occurs it is best to have the yearling shod. I have found it a good thing to put tips, or half shoes, on them. These tips should be countersunk in the wall of the foot so the bottom of the foot is level and at the proper angle to the ground.

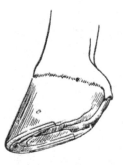

HALF SHOE OR TIP

In this way a horse can get the frog pressure which is so necessary if the foot is to be kept in a healthy condition. Proper frog pressure prevents contraction of the heels and tends to widen a narrow heel. It is rarely necessary to put shoes on a yearling's hind feet, and it is best to leave the hind shoes off as long as possible, because a kick from a bare foot is never as serious as one from a foot with a shoe on. There is another advantage in not having shoes on the hind feet: a horse playing in the paddock without hind shoes rarely grabs his front foot, which could cause a severe cut on the coronary band. And if he does grab himself, the injury will be mild as compared to one caused by a shod foot.

There should be a starting gate at a winter training grounds, as nearly as possible like the one used in racing. No opportunity should be missed in educating the yearlings in this contraption. Sometimes it may take a month to get a particular yearling to go into the gate. The obstinate ones should be coaxed and cajoled in every possible manner over a long period before any rough tactics are resorted to. A horse can easily be spoiled by improper teaching at this time. As soon as the yearlings learn that they have nothing to fear, they will go into the gate and stand quietly. They must be taught to walk into the gate, to walk through it, and to stand quietly, with the doors open in front of them at first. When they are sufficiently accustomed to the gate they must learn to stand quietly with the front doors closed. It is best to put the back bars in place immediately when the yearlings enter the gate, because one habit you do not want them to acquire is backing out, once they are in.

The routine of accustoming yearlings to the starting gate and gentling them while they are in it should be carried on all winter, weather permitting. The time to break young horses from the gate on the run comes after they are familiar with it in every way and you are actually preparing them to race.

When handling a yearling, talk to him and treat him as you would a child. An encouraging word expressed in a kindly tone, and a soft pat of the hand, are generally as well received by a young horse as by a human. A few minutes of kindness will pay big dividends in the later handling and training of these young animals.

A horse can easily be spoiled by improper teaching at this time . . . A few minutes of kindness will pay big dividends.
(Photo courtesy of Serita Hult)

Training 2-Year-Olds

The early training of 2-year-olds begins some time after the first of February and starts at a very gradual pace, just as they were handled at the outset of their training as yearlings. After a period of three or four weeks of long, slow gallops, which with most trainers means not less than 2 to 2 1/2 miles daily, including walking, jogging, and galloping, the 2-year-olds are ready for a bit of breezing, starting with a few quarter-miles in 26 to 27 seconds. Then comes three furlongs in 41 or 42 seconds, and several half-miles in 55 or 56 seconds. When the 2-year-olds have had enough of this, the trainer considers them fairly hard. He will increase their speed very gradually with some quarters in 24 seconds and three furlongs in 36 to 37 seconds, until they easily go a half-mile in 50 seconds. When my horses, young or old, have shown a half-mile in 50 seconds without any effort I always feel relieved, because I know that they have come through the early training period and are ready for a few serious works, which will put them in shape to start in a race. They have had enough foundation so a premature fast move will not hurt them, in case an exercise boy accidentally lets one of them go a bit faster than he is supposed to. After 2-year-olds have shown a half-mile in 50 seconds they are ready for some work at breaking fast.

Two-year-olds should be taught to break from a standing start. This is generally done at the starting gate, but they may receive their first lessons in flat-footed breaking before they are broken out of the gate. Flat-footed breaking should be taught only when there are few horses on the track, and it is better if the young horses can have the track to themselves, so accidents may be avoided. They should never be broken singly, but should be sent away in pairs, at least, and it is preferable to have three or four break together. They should always be started close to the inner rail. The boys should be instructed to keep them as straight as possible. The best way, at the beginning, is to walk the 2-year-olds for a step or two and break them together, at a signal. After they have broken this way once or twice they probably will break well from a standstill.

The early training of 2-year-olds . . . starts at a very gradual pace, just as they were handled at the onset of their training as yearlings.
(Photo courtesy of Thoroughbred Publications, Inc.)

This instruction will help them get out of the gate quickly. When they have learned how to break from a standstill, it will be much easier to get them to come out of the gate quickly. Horses schooled like this will require fewer lessons out of the gate and they will be less likely to injure themselves or a companion by swerving into the gate or into another horse. Most young horses will remember the lessons they received as yearlings, when they were taught to go into the gate and stand quietly. Two-year-olds that have not had this training as yearlings will have to go through a period of schooling as prescribed for yearlings. If a 2-year-old is to be raced early in the year, this preparation comes fairly early. However, no young horse should be put to this severe test until his trainer feels sure that he has had enough work so he can make the effort without hurting himself. Young horses should be broken from the gate as frequently as their behavior permits. Nervous, high-strung horses must be given a sufficient cooling-off period between lessons in breaking from the gate. When youngsters are calm enough to make a few starts from the gate at close intervals they will learn much faster. Some horses will show such aptitude for breaking that they will require only a few lessons. Once a horse has learned to leave the gate very fast, it is necessary only to give him periods of standing in the gate to be sure that he will behave properly when he is put in a race. It cannot be emphasized too much that breaking from the gate is a severe strain. The doors of the gate should be left open the first time or two that a young horse breaks from it. When a 2-year-old has had enough education in breaking to assure his trainer that he will behave in the gate and will break with his field, he is ready to make his first start, if his program calls for racing at that time.

It will be found that some of the more excitable horses will need to go back to the starting gate to be gentled until they stand quietly. This may also need to be repeated with some of them after their first race. Education in the gate cannot be hurried and it must be thorough, because what a horse learns in his early lessons affects his entire racing career.

Once a 2-year-old learns to race he is the toughest and truest machine we have in racing. A good 2-year-old will race very consistently. He will stand a lot of pounding in working and racing, but of course he can be overtaxed, which will affect his career as a 3-year-old. This applies to both colts and fillies, though colts are tougher than fillies and will stand more abuse. A filly that is raced hard, especially toward the end of her 2-year-old season, and goes into winter quarters light in flesh, will rarely put on any weight during the winter, and it will take a long time to bring her back to form as a 3-year-old.

A trainer should keep a daybook in which to set down particulars on every work done by his horses, including the weight carried, if it is worth noting, and the equipment used. In this way he can always refer to his records when he might be in doubt as to the fitness of his horse for a certain race, or if he wants to check on the equipment usually worn by the horse. He will also find the record most useful in looking up the final works preceding a horse's last successful race, in case it is considered desirable to give similar works for a coming race.

Barrier

Fifille ⎱ finished strong
Bold Beauty* ⎰
Big Flame ⎱ 5/8 mile 12¹-23⁴-35²-48⁶-1.02 (1.17'
Fixed Star ⎰ broke fast
broke slowly   1.04

Blue Hills ⎱ 3/4 · 12-23³ (36-50₀³
Why Not Now ⎰

The Peer Ⓐ ⎱ 5/8 Monmouth Barrier
Flaming Comet Ⓑ ⎰   " 12³-24³-36²-48-1.01²
Pilaya   '/4 "   .27³

1 - 1 - 3 - 4 $ 142,325.⁰⁰
20 - 20- 24- 22   2 stakes 6/25 incl.

The Dwyer
Young Away 121 Woodhouse 3rd 1/4- 2.07⁴ ✓ $ 5000.⁰⁰

Seaward 110 Jessop 3rd 1/8- 1.50⁴ ✓ 400.⁰⁰
Sussex Hdp.   equal record
Chanis 110 Jessop 2nd 1/4- 2.02 ✓ 5000.

Inseparable 113 Jessop 4th 1/4- 2.31² ✓ 400

Lucky Devil 109 Jessop 4th 3/4- 1.10⁴ ✓ 200

Mary Dyer Stakes
Black Chiffon 104 J. Renick 2nd -1.45³ ✓ 1500.

In the spring of the year a trainer with a number of 2-year-olds will select the small and very speedy ones for early racing, wisely reserving the big ones and the all-round better prospects for the important races later in the year. Some horses come to hand very quickly and can win a considerable amount before the less precocious ones are fit to race. This kind seems to run best at the shorter distances. If you don't take advantage of their speed for early races you miss out with them, because races for 2-year-olds stretch out beginning in the middle of the summer, and it is then that the better horses begin to show up.

An experienced trainer will quickly form an opinion as to the probable class of his young horses and will endeavor to keep them in their class. It will be found that if a horse is continually raced against horses that outclass him, he will go downhill until he won't be able to win at his own level. This is the same as a prizefighter being continually overmatched. He loses all heart and can't accomplish anything. At first they speak of him as a man who can take a lot of punishment, but the next thing you hear is that he is punch-drunk. Horses are pretty much like this. A man is very foolish to overmatch or over-race a 2-year-old who looks as if he may be a good prospect for racing at three, which is when the biggest purses are to be won.

Most 2-year-olds require strong riders, especially in the early part of their career. It takes a big, strong rider to get a 2-year-old away from the gate in a hurry and keep him going. Once they know what it's all about, the little boys can ride many of them, especially the fillies, who learn faster and are easier to handle once they are accustomed to racing.

A trainer should not hesitate to castrate a young horse when in his opinion he needs it. But he should do it only when he considers that the colt is not a good stallion prospect and when he feels sure that the alteration will make him a better race horse. I find that castration improves weedy colts and those with bad dispositions.

In giving a 2-year-old his final work for a race, I find it best to allow him two days between a fairly sharp move and the race. He then will have all his speed and will be alert, and will race much better than if handled in any other way. This pattern applies to fit horses. It must be remembered, however, that horses, like people, are all different, and one frequently finds a horse that requires much more work than the average. On the other hand there are quite a few horses on the delicate side who will not show their best in a race unless they are brought up to it on very light training. More Sun, whose works are shown at the end of this chapter along with Greek Ship's, was a horse who always got a sharp move the day before his race. I tried him the other way and found that he was such a glutton at the feed tub that he would fill up and blow very severely, so I concluded early in his 2-year-old form that he needed more and faster work than the average 2-year-old.

Two-year-olds are asked to go a distance of ground, up to 1 1/16 miles in this country, in the fall of the year. It will be found useful to breeze 2-year-olds a few times at distances from seven to eight furlongs in the autumn to determine which ones, if any, might be raced at the longer distances. As a rule, 2-year-olds can beat older horses in all-age races in the fall, and I have seen 2-year-olds win at a mile who later proved to be strictly sprinters and could not go a mile when they were older. In my opinion, distance racing does not hurt 2-year-olds unless it is overdone.

A 2-year-old that is to be raced over a distance for the first time should be educated to making the lower turn, starting from the grandstand. This can be difficult with some young horses because they are not accustomed to going around this turn at high speed. Their earlier racing has taught them that this is the place where they are generally taken to the middle of the track and eased up. It is an excellent idea to have an older horse who is used to running around this turn work on the outside of a young horse who is being educated to it.

As examples of the actual training of 2-year-olds, here are the works on More Sun and Greek Ship, covering December, 1948, when they were yearlings, and the early months of 1949, when they were two years old. Both colts won stakes later in the year. Only the work days are shown here. It may be assumed that the colts walked or galloped, according to what seemed best for them, between works.

| MORE SUN | GREEK SHIP |

DECEMBER, 1948, AT AIKEN, S.C.

1	3 furlongs, :40 3/5	2 furlongs, :28 1/5
4	3 furlongs, :39 3/5	2 furlongs, :25
7	3 furlongs, :38	3 furlongs, :39 3/5
10	3 furlongs, :12 2/5, :25, :38 1/5	3 furlongs, :11 4/5, 24 2/5, :37 4/5

Rainy and freezing weather interrupted any fast training at this point. Long gallops were given to each colt when the weather permitted, but there were no fast works. Both colts were wormed.

JANUARY, 1949

24 1 furlong, :13   1 furlong, :13
26 Both colts worked together, going a furlong in :12 1/5 and galloping out a
        quarter-mile in :24 3/5.
29 2 furlongs, :26   2 furlongs, :28 3/5

FEBRUARY

2 2 furlongs, :12 3/5, :24 4/5   2 furlongs, :12 2/5, :24 2/5
5 2 furlongs, :25 3/5   2 furlongs, :25 1/5
8 3 furlongs, :42 3/5   3 furlongs, :42 3/5
11 2 furlongs, :24 4/5, galloped out   2 furlongs, :24 2/5, galloped out 3
       3 furlongs in :38, and   furlongs in :38
       4 furlongs in :55
14 3 furlongs, :12 2/5, :24 4/5, :38 2/5, 3 furlongs, :12 3/5, :24 3/5, :39
17 2 furlongs, :13 1/5, :25 2/5, breaking 1 furlong, :13 2/5, galloping out 2 fur-
       from standing start   longs in :25 3/5, breaking from
                                           standing start
20 3 furlongs, :46   coughing, galloping but no breezing
                                           until March 9
25 2 furlongs from gate, :12, :23 4/5

MARCH

1 3 furlongs, :41 3/5
4 3 furlongs from barrier, :11 3/5,
       :24, :37
7 slow 4 furlongs, :56 3/5
9 coughing, gallop but no breezing   2 furlongs, :24 1/5

Because of a coughing epidemic at Aiken, the colts were restricted to slow galloping for the remainder of March. They were shipped to Belmont Park on March 31.

51

MORE SUN.   GREEK SHIP

                            APRIL

 3 gallop   3 furlongs, :43 3/5
 6 gallop   3 furlongs, :40 2/5
 9 gallop   3 furlongs, :38 3/5
12 gallop   3 furlongs, :12, :24, :37 2/5
13 2 furlongs, :27 1/5
15   4 furlongs, :52 3/5
16 3 furlongs, :40 3/5
18   3 furlongs, main track, :11 3/5, :23 2/5
                                      :36 1/5, galloped out 4 furlongs
                                      in :51 3/5 eased up

19 3 furlongs, :40
21   3 furlongs on main track, :12 1/5, :24 2/5,
                                      :36 3/5, galloped out 4 furlongs,
                                      :49 4/5, eased up 5 furlongs, 1:04 3/5

22 4 furlongs, :53 1/5
24   3 furlongs on main track, standing
                                      start, :12 2/5, :24 1/5, :36 1/5,
                                      galloped out 4 furlongs, :50 1/5

25 3 furlongs, :13, :25, :37 2/5, gal-
       loped out 4 furlongs in :51 2/5
27   3 furlongs, :12 3/5, :24 2/5, :36 3/5,
                                      galloped out 4 furlongs in :50

28 4 furlongs from standing start,
       13 4/5, :26 2/5, :39 3/5, :53 1/5
30   4 furlongs from the gate, :12 2/5,
                                      :24 1/5, 36 3/5, :49 1/5, galloped
                                      out 5 furlongs in 1:03 3/5

MAY

1   3 furlongs from standing start
        :13, :25, :37, galloped out
        4 furlongs in :50 2/5, 5 fur-
        longs in 1:04

3   4 furlongs, sloppy track, :11 4/5, :24 1/5,
                                                                36 2/5, :49 2/5

4   4 furlongs from barrier, slow
        track, :12 3/5, :24 3/5,
        :36 3/5, :49 3/5

6   3 furlongs from barrier, :12, :23 2/5,
                                                                :35 3/5, galloped out 4 furlongs in
                                                                :49, 5 furlongs in 1:04 4/5

7   4 furlongs from barrier, sloppy
        track, :12 2/5, :24 4/5,
        :35 4/5, :49 3/5

9   2 furlongs, :27 3/5

10 Both colts were worked together down the Widener chute at Belmont Park,
        over a sloppy track - :12 3/5, :24 1/5, :36 2/5, :48 4/5

13 Both colts worked together, 2 furlongs, :12 2/5, :23 3/5, eased up
        3 furlongs in :36 4/5

14 More Sun won first start, 4 1/2 furlongs
        in :52, at Belmont Park

15 walked

16 galloped   3 furlongs, :12, :23, :35, galloped
                                                                out 4 furlongs in :48 2/5

17 3 furlongs, :39

18 Third to Ferd and Navy Chief in
        Juvenile Stakes, beaten neck
        and head, 5 furlongs in :57 4/5

19   Greek Ship fourth in first start, beat-
                                                                en about 2 1/2 lengths in :59 2/5

22 Both colts worked together, sloppy track, 3 furlongs in :38 1/5, galloped
        out 4 furlongs in :53 1/5

23   Greek Ship won his second start,
                                                                beating Detective and Shock,
                                                                5 furlongs, :59

Later in the year More Sun, a chestnut colt by Sun Again - The Damsel, by Flag Pole, won the Graduation Stakes, The United States Hotel Stakes, and the Saratoga Special, was second in the colt division of the National Stallion Stakes and was third in the Juvenile and the Flash Stakes. Greek Ship, a brown colt by *Heliopolis - Boat, by Man o' War, won the Wakefield, Flash, and Mayflower Stakes and was third in the Albany Handicap.

MORE SUN winning the U.S. Hotel Stakes at Saratoga, 1949.
(Photo courtesy of Thoroughbred Publications, Inc.)

3-Year-Olds and Older Horses

OCCASIONALLY, if they show sufficient promise, 2-year-olds are put by early, sometimes in September, so they may race in the classics at three. There were several examples of that among the 2-year-olds of 1951. Cousin and Primate were given their last races as 2-year-olds in the Futurity Stakes at Belmont Park on October 6. Tom Fool made only one start after winning the Futurity, when he won the East View Stakes on October 24. These colts, with Hill Gail, were rated among the top half-dozen 2-year-olds of 1951. Hill Gail was taken to California after the Futurity and although he was winter-raced, he did not start for three months, until January 5, when he raced at six furlongs, and was prepared, by workouts and races at gradually increasing distances, for the Santa Anita Derby of February 23, which he won. Later he won the Kentucky Derby. Primate was trained during the winter at Hialeah Park. Cousin was winter-trained in California. Tom Fool got his winter rest period and preparation for spring racing at Aiken, S. C. Tom Fool, Primate, and Cousin made their first starts of 1952 in New York on April 7, racing in top form at six furlongs.

A 3-year-old being prepared for the classics (Kentucky Derby, Preakness, Belmont Stakes) should be well seasoned by long, slow gallops if he was not raced during the winter. This preparation should continue until the first or the middle of February, when the horse should start off with several slow breezes at two and three furlongs. His work continues at a slow pace until he goes six furlongs in 1:22 to 1:25, when it is well to go back to one of the shorter distances, possibly four furlongs, which will be breezed in 51 or 52 seconds. He then should be ready for a half in 50 seconds. From there he can be stretched out to six furlongs in 1:20. Then he will go back to three furlongs in 35 1/2 or 36 seconds. This will be followed by slow moves up to six furlongs in 1:18. Now the horse should be ready for a fairly sharp five furlongs, in about 1:01 or a little faster, depending on the track. His next move could be seven furlongs in 1:32. After this he would be ready to go a sharp four furlongs, in company, from the starting gate. This amount of training would require a total of some six or seven weeks.

The idea is to never give a horse a speedy work until you are sure that he has had a proper foundation of slow work to make him physically fit for the faster move. A very fast move by an unfit horse will sometimes put him off his feed and completely knock him out physically for quite a while.

After the long, slow preparation referred to, the horse should be up to starting in a six-furlong race. Following this he can be breezed several slow miles and possibly be started in the Experimental Free Handicap No. 2, at 1 1/16 miles, or in a condition race prior to the 1 1/8-mile Wood Memorial. If he has been sent to Kentucky, he may start in the 1 1/8-mile Blue Grass Stakes at Keeneland.

If you are going to start a horse in the Kentucky Derby it is a good idea to have him down there in time to get a good work about a week before the race. If you think he would do better for having a race over the Churchill Downs track, he should get there in time for a little breeze or blowout before the one-mile Derby Trial, and get his track feeler in that race.

Horses that race in the Derby and start right back in the Preakness generally get one useful move over the Pimlico track, a few days before the race. Following the Derby and the Preakness, the third of the classics for 3-year-olds is the 1 1/2-mile Belmont Stakes. If you want to give your horse a race over the Belmont track there are several prep races he can run in, for example the Withers Stakes, at a mile, and the Peter Pan Handicap, at 1 1/8 miles.

All in all, a 3-year-old is pretty busy, competing for such a succession of golden prizes. In preparing a horse for such a series of races, a trainer must know his horse. He must know how much he can stand, and how much work he requires. A few oats left in the feed box at dinner time will tell a trainer that the program is a little too strenuous and that he had better miss an engagement or at least ease up a bit on the work.

On the other hand, if a horse eats gluttonously, stops a little in his work, and blows hard after each work, the trainer can be sure that this fellow's training and racing program is not hurting him. Possibly increased work should be considered in such a case.

As for training a horse for a long race, the real distance races come in the autumn. It is not necessary to give a horse a trial over the full distance of a coming race. A mile and a half is far enough to work a horse for any of the present-day distance races. We have learned recently that a sharp, speedy move close to a race is better for a horse than a long, hard work. I observed years ago that Gwyn Tompkins, one of the best trainers of steeplechasers I ever knew, worked some of his horses a speedy half-mile the day before they were to compete in a jumping event of from 2 to 2 1/2 miles. I saw Weldship win several top races when trained in this fashion. He was a big, stout, heavy horse and would never go fast over a long distance in his training. A sharp half-mile, generally in 48 seconds, the day before a race would put him on edge and he would win his race, going to the front immediately and sticking it out after making the pace for the entire distance.

A horse of Weldship's type might require a similar fast move the day before a race even though he might be prepping for a shorter flat race. All these things should be thought out by the trainer, who should study his horses carefully. He soon learns the ones that require a stiff work before a race and those who would be knocked out by such a work and, as they express it on the Turf, "leave his race on the track."

Geldings almost invariably require less work than stallions. This applies more especially after they are 2-year-olds. A great many fillies race well off light training, but occasionally one finds a filly who is an exceptionally good feeder and who appears quite masculine in every way. Such a filly may require and take as much or more fast work than a sturdy colt.

BOLD

Here is the course of preparation undergone by Bold, who won the 1951 Preakness for the Brookmeade Stable. Bold was troubled with splints, bucked shins, and sore feet, and moreover was a difficult colt to restrain in his works. However, he had exceptional speed, as some of the workouts indicate. He usually was walked the day after a work, then was galloped until the next workout. Up to January 1 he had received a course of long gallops and slow breezes.

JANUARY, 1951, AT HIALEAH PARK

3 3 furlongs, :41
7 3 furlongs, :39 3/5
10 4 furlongs, :53
13 5 furlongs, 1:08 4/5
16 3 furlongs, :41
19 5 furlongs, 1:09
22 6 furlongs, 1:23 4/5
25 3 furlongs, :37 2/5
28 6 furlongs, :12 3/5, :24 3/5, :37 3/5, :50 4//5, 1:04, 1:18 4/5. Bold was inclined to bear out during this workout, and was hard to control. He worked a bit too fast for the stage of preparation he was in.
31 A one-cup blinker was tried on Bold, but he still was hard to hold, and showed an inclination to bear out slightly. 4 furlongs, :12 3/5, :24 3/5, :36 4/5, :49 2/5

FEBRUARY

3 7 furlongs, :13 3/5, :26 3/5, :38 3/5, :51 1/5, 1:04, 1:16 3/5, 1:31
6 6 furlongs, :13 2/5, :25 1/5, :37 2/5, :50, 1:02 2/5, 1:17 1/5, eased up
10 7 furlongs, 1:34
13 5 furlongs, :12 1/5, :24 1/5, :37 3/5, bore out, pulled up 5 furlongs, 1:06
16 2 furlongs, :25. Runout bit was used.
17 3 furlongs, :11 4/5, :23 4/5, 35 2/5. Bolted, though runout bit was used.
19 Because of bruised feet, Bold was shipped to Aiken. His shoes were pulled off and he was galloped up to about 2 miles a day, going the reverse way on the deep, 5-furlong sandy training track. When he was trained the reverse way of the track he did not bear out. On March 19 he resumed breezing.

MARCH

19 4 furlongs, barefoot, reverse way of 5-furlong training track, :56 2/5
22 5 furlongs, 1:10
25 6 furlongs, 1:26 1/5
28 4 furlongs, :24 1/2, :49 3/5. This was considered an unusually fast move over this old, deep track.
31 6 furlongs, 1:22

APRIL

4   2 furlongs, :24 3/5

5   5 furlongs, reverse way of mile track at Aiken, 11 4/5, :22 4/5, :34 3/5, :47 4/5,
      1:01 2/5. Tired badly. It was intended that he work in 1:03, but the boy
      couldn't hold him during the first part of the work.

8   4 furlongs, :50

10 7 furlongs, 1:34. Shipped to Belmont Park in the afternoon.

12 galloped

13 galloped

14 Belmont Park training track, reverse way, 4 furlongs, :12 3/5, :25 2/5, :36 3/5, :48 2/5,
      galloped out 5 furlongs in 1:03 4/5, pulled up. Bold's preparation was in view
      of the Toboggan Handicap. Until his work of May 1 (see below), the Toboggan
      was his immediate goal.

17 1 mile, reverse way, :14 3/5, :27, :41, :54, 1:07 2/5, 1:19 4/5, 1:31 4/5, 1:45 2/5, galloped
      out 9 furlongs, pulled up in 2:01. It was intended that he work the mile in 1:50.

21 4 furlongs, reverse way, :12 4/5, :24 2/5, :36 3/5, :49, 5 furlongs pulled up in 1:03.

24 6 furlongs, reverse way, :12, :23 1/5, :35, :47, 1:00, 1:13, eased up 7 furlongs, 1:27 2/5.

27 3 furlongs, reverse way, :12 1/5, :23 1/5, :36 1/5.

30 2 furlongs, reverse way, :12 2/5, :24, sloppy track.

MAY

1   1 mile, right way of track, 122 pounds up, :12 4/5, :24 3/5, :36 3/5, :49, 1:01 4/5, 1:14,
      1:27, 1:40 2/5, eased up 9 furlongs in 1:55 4/5. Boy had been instructed to
      go the mile in 1:46 or 1:47. This work led to the decision to start Bold in
      the Preakness. It proved to me that the horse was fit and that instead of
      racing in the 6-furlong Toboggan, a longer distance was to his liking.

4   Main track, 5 furlongs, one-cup blinker, right way of track, in company, from
      starting gate, :12, :24, :35 2/5, :46 3/5, :59, eased up 6 furlongs in 1:12,
      beating workmate by 5 or 6 lengths.

7   Shipped to Pimlico to get a race over the track and receive his final prep for the
      Preakness.

8   3 furlongs, :11 3/5, :22 4/5, :35, eased up 4 furlongs in :47 3/5. Was supposed to go
      3 furlongs in :37.

9   First start of year, 1 1/16 miles, allowance race for 3-year-olds, won by 12 lengths
      in 1:45, beating six other horses.

13 3 furlongs, :11 2/5, :23, :35, eased up 4 furlongs in :48 2/5. Was intended to go 3
        furlongs at a much slower pace.

14 Preakness Prep Purse, 1 1/16 miles, beaten a neck by Alerted in 1:43 3/5. Sonic
        third. The jockey's ride on Bold was considered one of his poorer efforts.

15 Shoes pulled off because of sore feet. Walked.
16 Walked.
17 Galloped barefoot. Shod that afternoon.
18 5 furlongs, :11 4/5, :23 1/5, :35, :47 4/5, eased up 5 furlongs in 1:02.
19 Won 1 3/16 mile Preakness by 7 lengths, leading all the way. Counterpoint second,
        Alerted third. Wore one-cup blinker, which he always wore when racing
        or working the right way of the track. After the Preakness, Bold was returned
        to Belmont Park. He ran out in a prep race for the Belmont Stakes and was
        found to be suffering from a sore shin and a sore splint. In the summer of 1952,
        when he was nearly ready to return to racing, Bold was killed by lightning while in
        a paddock at the farm.

ASSAULT

Through the courtesy of my friend Max Hirsch, one of the top trainers of today, the works on the King Ranch's Assault have been made available for 1946, the year he won the American Triple Crown. It will be noted that Bold and Assault were trained differently, according to their individual needs. Assault's program was directed toward fitting him for the stress of a long campaign, with emphasis on speed during the latter part of a race. The son of Bold Venture - Igual, by Equipoise, earned $424,195 in 1946, when he was a 3-year-old, which at the time was a record for a single year. This was accomplished despite an illness during the summer which interrupted his training and racing.

Assault was galloped all winter at Columbia, S. C., and was turned out each afternoon, weather permitting. He began slow breezes toward the end of January. Between works he was walked or galloped, according to what his trainer considered necessary.

JANUARY, 1946, AT COLUMBIA

21 1 furlong, :14
23 1 furlong, :13 3/5
25 2 furlongs, :27

28 2 furlongs, :29
30 2 furlongs, :27

FEBRUARY

3 4 furlongs, :54
6 4 furlongs, :54
9 4 furlongs, :54
12 6 furlongs, 1:22
15 6 furlongs, 1:22
18 8 furlongs, 1:50

21 4 furlongs, :52
22 8 furlongs, 1:48
24 3 furlongs, :37
25 8 furlongs, 1:47
28 4 furlongs, :54

MARCH

1 4 furlongs, :50 2/5
4 3 furlongs, :41, in company
5 5 furlongs, 1:07
8 3 furlongs, :38
10 5 furlongs, 1:06
15 3 furlongs, :38
18 4 furlongs, :52

21 4 furlongs, :51 2/5
23 6 furlongs, :14 1/5, :29 2/5, :41,
    :55, 1:20, (last quarter in :25)
26 3 furlongs, :37 1/5
27 8 furlongs, 1:49 2/5
30 3 furlongs, :35 3/5, fast work for
    Columbia track

APRIL

1 Shipped to Belmont Park
5 3 furlongs, :37
6 6 furlongs, 1:14
9 First start of year. Won Experi-
    mental Free Handi-
    cap No. 1, 6 furlongs
    in 1:12, by 4 1/2 lengths
12 4 furlongs, :48 2/5
14 3 furlongs, 35 1/5
15 8 furlongs, :13, :26 2/5, :39 1/5,
    :52 3/5, 1:06, 1:19 3/5,
    1:43 4/5 (last quarter
    in :24 1/5)

18 8 furlongs, 1:41 2/5
20 Second start, won Wood Memorial,
    1 1/16 miles in 1:46 3/5,
    by 2 1/4 lengths.
23 3 furlongs, :39. Shipped to
    Churchill Downs.
27 8 furlongs, 1:42
30 Derby Trial Stakes, 1 mile, 1:40 1/5,
    muddy track, finished fourth.

MAY

3	4 furlongs :48
4	Won Kentucky Derby, 1 1/4 miles, by eight lengths in 2:06 3/5, sloppy track.
5	Walked
6	Shipped to Pimlico
8	3 furlongs, :10
9	8 furlongs, 1:45
11	Won Preakness Stakes, 1 3/16 miles, by a neck in 2:01 2/5, fast track.
12	Shipped to Belmont Park
16	4 furlongs, :52
18	3 furlongs, :40
20	4 furlongs, :48
22	8 furlongs, 1:43 3/5
24	3 furlongs, :35
25	1 1/4 miles, :50, 1:15, 1:40, 2:05
28	4 furlongs, :50
29	1 1/2 miles, 2:32

JUNE

1	Won Belmont Stakes, 1 1/2 miles by 3 lengths in 2:30 4/5, fast track.
5	4 furlongs, :52
7	4 furlongs :51
9	8 furlongs 1:43
11	3 furlongs, :36
13	8 furlongs, 1:43, at Aqueduct
15	Won Dwyer Stakes, 1 1/4 miles, by 4 1/2 lengths in 2:06 4/5, fast track
18	3 furlongs, :40
20	4 furlongs, :51
24	4 furlongs, :48
29	3 furlongs, :39
30	4 furlongs, :50

JULY

3	3 furlongs, :37
7	6 furlongs 1:19
9	8 furlongs, 1:45 2/5
12	8 furlongs, 1:47

The remainder of the works for Assault in July were not kept on the regular sheet and are not available. On July 27, his next start, Assault was beaten to sixth in the 1 1/4-mile Arlington Classic, won by The Dude in 2:02 3/5. Assault appeared to be lame in his right hind leg after the race, but later the trouble was diagnosed as a kidney ailment. He did not race again until September 7, but was kept in light training throughout August.

AUGUST

4	4 furlongs, :50 2/5
6	4 furlongs, :50
9	4 furlongs, :50
12	4 furlongs, :50
14	6 furlongs, 1:22
16	4 furlongs, :49 3/5
20	4 furlongs, :51 2/5
23	5 furlongs, 1:08 2/5
26	6 furlongs, 1:19
28	6 furlongs, 1:18

3 3 furlongs, :35
5 8 furlongs, 1:42 3/5
7 Third to Mighty Story and Ma-
     hout in 1 1/8-mile
     Discovery Handicap
10 3 furlongs, :37
11 8 furlongs, 1:40 3/5
14 Second to Mahout in 1 1/8-
     mile Jersey Handicap.

19 4 furlongs, :51
21 8 furlongs, 1:40 3/5
23 8 furlongs, 1:38 2/5
25 Dead heat for third with Flare-
     back in 1 1/2-mile Manhattan
     Handicap. Stymie first,
     Pavot second

OCTOBER

2 3 furlongs, :40
3 4 furlongs, :52
5 4 furlongs, :50
8 4 furlongs, :51
10 6 furlongs, 1:15 3/5
13 3 furlongs, :36 2/5
14 6 furlongs, 1:15
17 8 furlongs, 1:40 3/5

19 Second to Bridal Flower in
     1 3/16-mile Roamer Handicap.
22 4 furlongs, :49
23 1 1/2 miles, 1:15, 1:40, 2:31
25 3 furlongs, :38
26 Third to Stymie and *Rico
     Monte in 1 5/8-mile Gallant
     Fox Handicap.
29 3 furlongs, :38

NOVEMBER

1 Won the 1 3/16-mile Pimlico Special,
     1:57, fast track, with Ar-
     caro up instead of Merh-
     tens, the regular rider.
4 3 furlongs, :39
6 8 furlongs, 1:45

8 3 furlongs, :37
9 Won 1 3/16-mile Westchester Han-
     dicap, 1:56 2/5, fast track,
     Arcaro up
Shipped to Columbia for the winter.

Assault's second race as a 3-year-old brought as easy victory in the Wood Memorial Stakes, in April.
(Bert Morgan Photo courtesy of Keeneland Association)

OLDER HORSES

Four-year-olds and older horses are brought out of their winter rest period in the same manner as prescribed for three-year-olds. They are given a term of long, slow gallops, then are started breezing slow quarter-miles, three-eighths, and half-miles. Horses 3 years old and upward that also have raced the previous year and who come out for their first race in the spring are sometimes extremely nervous and washy, and take a lot out of themselves in the saddling paddock before a race. Now and then this over-anxiety uses up all their energy before they are ready to break out of the starting gate. Some of this can be averted by taking a horse to the paddock to see the crowds and get the feel of things a few days before he is to make his first start of the year. If it seems necessary, this can be repeated.

Most older horses do not require as much work as younger ones. Those with such ailments as bad feet, ankles, knees, and so on should receive any necessary hard work well in advance of a race. Then they should be trained lightly up to the race, so any soreness which might have come from the stiff work will have time to subside. Most sore horses train better over a deep or sandy track. A very good example of such a track is the one called "Oklahoma," at Saratoga Springs. There is an exception to this rule - a horse with sore knees trains better on a track that is firm but not too hard. A cuppy track that breaks away from a sore-kneed horse puts too much strain on his knees.

When a horse develops something seriously wrong, such as a bowed tendon, or bunchy knees that cause such lameness that his training cannot be continued, or a broken sesamoid bone, or a broken bone in a foot, he is best sent to the farm and turned out for something like a year. Some treatment may be started before he is sent to the farm, and continued after his arrival there. This will depend on the type of injury. Treatments for different ailments may vary considerably, but there isn't much that can be done about any serious injury until the fever and soreness have disappeared. The horse then can be treated and turned out on grass. Subsequent treatment or medication can be carried out under the supervision of a veterinarian or someone else experienced with such things. It is the time element that really does the good. Treatment helps, but Nature, in the main, is the final healer.

The training of an injured horse, when he is put under saddle again, is about the same as for any horse of his age, with the exception that he requires more careful watching. I might state right here that the trainer or his assistant should carefully examine the feet and legs of every horse in the stable, sound or unsound, every day. In the case of horses that have been injured and are being brought back to racing after a period of rest and treatment, the slightest fever in the injured member should be considered a red light. Stop training until the fever has subsided.

Fever in a leg or a foot, just as in the body, is Nature's first warning that something is not quite right. We take a horse's body temperature to check his general welfare, and we feel his feet and legs

65

to see if he is sound. Many a trainer would have averted a bad breakdown if he had heeded the first warning and stopped work with his horse until the trouble that was brewing had been taken care of by treatments or rest.

The early training of horses that come back to racing after having been injured is naturally at a slower pace than for sound horses, because of the precautions that must be taken. Try not to give them any stiff work on a bad or slippery track. This applies especially to horses with bowed tendons.

There is an old saying that one race is better than several works. This means that most horses get something out of a race that you cannot give them in a work. Of course it is to be understood that a horse must be fit enough to stand the pressure of a hard race. He may get a strenuous race even though you want him to have a comparatively easy one the first time out, because a lot of unforeseen things can come up during a race. A race may look easy on paper, but there are such things as a horse getting a very poor start, or perhaps running up against a tough racer who shows unexpectedly improved form.

Mud Horses, Grass Horses and Steeplechasers

SOME HORSES are natural mud runners. They can run on any type of muddy track. There are other horses that race well only when a track has a watery surface and a firm bottom, which is called a sloppy track. Other horses prefer deep, heavy mud. A great many sore horses race better when the track is a little on the slow, soft side. Some horses do not like any sort of muddy track. However, I have seen horses learn to race well in the mud when, because of rain over a long period, they had nothing but mud to train and race in. I noticed this particularly one winter when I raced at New Orleans. Looking back at that winter, I can remember nothing but muddy tracks.

No one knows what makes a mudder or a non-mudder. I think that mud calks on shoes help a horse racing in the mud, because they keep him from slipping. I feel that often it is the fear of slipping that causes a horse to be a non-mudder. Mud calks could give him confidence. A stallion who has raced well in the mud often sires successful mud runners. But even though at times the offspring of certain stallions seem to be capable mudders, an exception will be found occasionally in a horse by such a sire who cannot, as the saying goes, untrack himself in the mud.

One well-known handicapper tried to pick mud runners by watching the horses walk in the paddock before a race. He would take a chance on the ones that set their toes down firmly, as if digging in, before putting down their heels. He claimed that the ones that put their feet down toe-first would get better traction in the mud than the ones who landed on their heels first and therefore were more likely to slip and slide. However, I am sure that the answer as to why a horse can or cannot run in the mud will never be discovered.

Racing on grass is a different proposition, although it may be noted that good mud horses generally race well on the turf. My experience has been that horses with high action race better on turf than those with low, smooth action. The latter type of horse does not go well over grass. In England they call them "daisy-cutters." Several of our great old jumpers had bad action for flat racing but were well suited to racing over turf. A horse that goes over the grass with high action does better than a daisy-cutter because he strides over the grass rather than through it, and thus meets with less resistance. It is natural that a horse whose low action keeps his feet continually brushing through the grass will be impeded to a certain extent.

No one knows what makes a mudder.
(Photo by Francis Routt, courtesy of Maryland Horse)

Recently I raced Greek Ship over the grass without any advance preparation or any knowledge as to whether or not he would like it.

He is a horse with good action and is not one that I would pick out as a particularly good grass performer. In his case the reason I selected grass racing was that he had shown a decided dislike for having dirt thrown in his face, and I thought he might like racing over the grass, where comparatively little dirt is thrown. I also knew, of course, that he had shown good form in the mud at various times.

Horses with high action may prefer turf.
(Photo courtesy of Thoroughbred Publications, Inc.)

I think that very often the reason imported horses, especially those coming from England, do not race well over our dirt tracks is because they have always trained and raced on grass courses and have not been subjected to having dirt thrown in their faces. Our American horses race and train over dirt tracks and become used to it. I understand that in South America they have both dirt and grass tracks, and more of these horses seem to adapt themselves to our racing than those coming from England.

TRAINING HORSES TO JUMP

The first step in teaching horses to jump is to train them to get over whatever obstacle may be in their path. The best way to start them is in a specially built corral containing two or more jumps, according to the size of the corral. As a rule these corrals are circular, with a high board fence on the outside and the jumps on the inside. The jumps are five or six feet wide. A lower panel fence is built inside the jumps. The inner and outer fences form a lane in which the horse is schooled over the obstacles. The footing in such a corral should be firm, but not too hard. Sand is very good if it isn't too deep.

A horse's first lessons should be over small obstacles. If you have several jumps inside the corral they can be constructed of various materials, such as rails, hedge, logs, etc. The jumps must be spaced far enough apart to permit a horse to take at least half a dozen strides between obstacles. The horse is generally led in without a rider, for his first lessons. He is walked up to the first jump and allowed to examine it, then is taken back far enough to allow him to get into his stride before he reaches the obstacle. Then he is turned toward the jump and started off, usually at the crack of a whip. It is best to have a man in the center ring of the corral with a long whip. The man should be careful at the outset to crack his whip only when he is behind the horse, be-cause if he is alongside him or slightly in front of him he can very easily cause the horse to wheel before reaching the jump.

The idea is to teach the horse to go ahead when he sees a jump. It is surprising how quickly horses learn what you want them to do. Frequently you will find a horse who is so keen and eager to jump that you have to prevent him from overdoing. During the early lessons without a rider up, a horse should wear a bridle, and it is just as well to have a saddle on him too. The stirrups should be slid up to the top of the stirrup webbing and the bridle reins should be tucked under the stirrups.

If a horse is thought to be sufficiently clever at jumping after several lessons with just the saddle and bridle on him, a boy can be put on his back in the corral. The jumps are usually constructed so a horse can go over them in either direction. It is a great help to a horse if he is sent four or five turns around the corral in one direction and then sent in the reverse direction. Before starting him in the other direction, let him have a breather if he is winded. The height of the jumps should be increased gradually until the horse is going over fairly normal jumps. When a trainer feels that his horse has been sufficiently educated in the corral, he can be given some lessons over a regular jumping course. At most places where there is any amount of jumping there will be a special schooling course for beginners. The obstacles on this course will not be quite as high as those on the racing course.

It is surprising how quickly horses learn.
(*Mike Sirico photo, courtesy of NYRA*)

A quiet and capable older fencer is a great help in giving a green horse a lead while he is learning. When green horses are sufficiently schooled they generally are sent over the fences in pairs. Their training on the flat is about the same as for any flat racer, except that a school over the fences frequently takes the place of what would be a work for a flat horse.

A horse's schooling in jumping may be started at any age, although there are no races for jumpers until about the middle of their 3-year-old year. A 3-year-old jumper should be raced very sparingly. Some of the more successful stables do not race their horses over jumps until they are 4-year-olds. By then they are jumping more proficiently and are much more tractable and better developed physically. The early training and racing of some horses begins over hurdles. If they show an aptitude for the bigger jumps they are put to steeplechasing later. Training them for hurdle racing is easier and a shorter preparation is required.

I like to shoe jumpers with long, sharp calks on the outside of the hind shoes. This prevents their sliding on their hind quarters, which jumpers often do when landing after clearing a fence.

Thomas Hitchcock, who was considered by many persons to be the best handler of jumping horses in this country, very often selected horses for his jumping stable when they were yearlings, or even as weanlings. He began immediately to let them know what they had to do in order to get over an obstacle in their path. He would place small obstacles at the gates to the paddocks and pastures where they were turned out. They jumped these when entering and leaving the fields. As he was one of the most successful men we have ever had in steeplechasing in America, his methods must have been exceptionally good.

It is not absolutely necessary, however, to start jumping lessons early in a horse's life. Frequently a horse that has been purchased after having raced on the flat for several years will become a top jumping horse.

It is just as natural for a horse to jump as it is for a man to jump, but some horses, like some people, can jump better and with less exertion than others. A good schooling boy is most invaluable because a horse can easily be spoiled by an inexperienced or incompetent rider. A rider who schools jumpers must be confident and fearless. This applies even more to jumping horses than to horses trained for flat racing.

Boots are an important item in the equipment of a jumping stable. There are bell boots to protect a young horse's quarters when he is learning to jump. There are shin boots to protect the hind shins, and some trainers never send a horse out for schooling without putting a good pair of boots on his front legs. The front boots and hind shin boots are usually made of strong felt, with a little padding. Blinkers are often useful on a jumping horse, especially if he is inclined to go into his fences in a hesitating, swerving manner.

The Condition Book

WHEN looking over a condition book and picking spots for my horses, I always think of my good friend Phil Chinn. When asked the secret of his success in racing (and in the old days he really had success on the race track, although in recent years he has been better known as a breeder), his reply was: "I always put my horses in the worst company I can find for them and keep myself in the best company I can find."

It takes intelligence to read today's condition books. In the old days they were much more simply written. Today a racing secretary works harder and longer over his condition book, and he puts in many a little catch that will get your horse in over his head if you aren't careful. When you have a maiden, the answer is very simple: put him in a maiden race. People will sometimes object to this, saying that their horses are good enough to beat other than maidens, and they put them in allowance races where they meet winners. Sometimes it is done because a horse is fit and there is no maiden race on the program at that time; or his handler may do this to get him into a smaller field; or in some rare cases a man will do this to get a price on his maiden and win a bet.

However, if you put a maiden in an allowance race your horse will frequently be beaten, because he will meet horses that have won or have had more experience. If your maiden does win an allowance race, you will discover later that the victory has penalized him, because certain races may offer allowances for non-winners of other than a maiden race. Your horse therefore will not be eligible for this weight concession.

After a horse has won a maiden race his next likely spot is in a race for non-winners of two races. When he has won two races he will be eligible for many races written for horses that have not won two races other than maiden, or as the conditions generally read, "other than maiden or claiming."

As for fillies, there are times, more especially in their 2-year-old form, when they can beat the colts. If it is a question of winning a bet, you may win with a particularly fast filly in an open maiden race and get better odds on her than in a race restricted to fillies. Better odds can be had on a filly in an open race because there is an old saying that colts can beat fillies. Most people believe this, and will bet on a colt against a filly. But very often one sees a 2-year-old filly who can beat the colts. Fillies have the knack of breaking quicker out of the gate. Of course in a race that requires strength and stamina, the colts will usually beat the fillies. You will find a number of 2-year-old fillies on the winning roster of the Futurity Stakes, but when it comes to races for 3-year-olds, like the Belmont Stakes, only the fillies Ruthless and Tanya are listed as winners. However, following the advice of my friend Colonel Chinn, I believe that a trainer has greater success with his fillies if he keeps them in mare and filly races. It is only now and then that a trainer will have an exceptional mare who can be pitted against the colts and beat them. The reason for racing her against colts is the lack of opportunity for such a mare to race entirely against horses of her own sex. In spite of efforts to increase the opportunities for fillies and mares, there are comparatively few races exclusively for them.

Selling platers should be very carefully placed. Horses worth $5,000 should be kept in their class; $7,500 horses should be kept in their class, and so on. There are times when a horse may win if raced a notch or two above his real level, but in the long run a trainer who knows how to evaluate a horse and race him only against those of equal caliber will be the most successful manager. The mere fact of losing a race may not appear serious to a layman, but experience over a long period has proven that a horse that is continually sent against better horses will become so discouraged that he can't win any kind of a race. By contrast, horses for whom easy spots have been found, enabling them to win several consecutive races, gain in courage and confidence and often go on to better things.

A trainer's records should be so complete that he can determine very quickly just what horse he has whose winnings or non-winnings make him fit the conditions for certain races. It is easy to remember maidens and winners of one race, but the eligibility conditions for other horses become much more complicated. For example, if a condition book contains a race for "4-year-olds and upward, non-winners of $3,500 twice in 1951-52 or two races other than claiming since March 4," a trainer has to turn to his record book to be sure that his horse is eligible. Trainers of small stables do not have so much trouble on this score, but the trainer of a large number of horses cannot carry everything in his head.

The need for accurate and complete records also applies to the claiming of weight allowances. A race may read: "non-winners of $2,000 three times since October 20 allowed three pounds; of four races since September 15 or a race since March 20, six pounds; of $3,500 at any time or a race since January 16, nine pounds; of a race since November 20, 12 pounds; since October 1, 15 pounds (claiming races not considered)." To get the necessary information, a trainer must turn to his record book. Some racing secretaries make special allowances in addition to the usual conditions, as "non-winners at a mile or over when racing at a mile or over if 3-year-olds three pounds, if four-year-olds and up five pounds." In my opinion, a rule could be made to provide for such allowances. I think it would be useful to both the racing secretaries and the horsemen. It is allowances races at a mile or more that are the hardest to fill. A rule granting weight concessions of this kind would encourage more entries in these races. Often a trainer, if encouraged to start a horse in such a race, will discover that a horse he has considered to be a sprinter will actually go a distance, and the racing secretary thus gains another horse to help fill his distance races. It is for this reason that I say that a detailed record book must be kept, giving the statistics on all horses in the stable.

The rules of racing state that the owner (and by extension, the trainer) is responsible for the weight carried by his horse. This means that if you enter a horse too light, claiming an allowance to which you are not entitled, your horse may be disqualified. On the other hand, if you don't claim an allowance that your horse ought to get, and you thereby lose a race because of the extra poundage, then you may be put down as just plain stupid.

In regard to weights, a trainer may find that certain of his horses race better with light weight. For these horses he must select races in which they will carry light weight. But if he has a good weight-carrier he may gain an advantage in picking a race where all the horses must carry heavy weights. There probably will be some horses in there that will not like the heavy weight and will be at a disadvantage, enabling his horse to race under more favorable conditions.

I always try to get a jockey who can make the weight assigned to my horse. Even one pound overweight may cost a race. There are times when you do have to carry a little overweight, but I rarely ever enter in a race where I cannot take advantage of all the allowances my horse is entitled to. Carrying overweight is a disadvantage to a horse that you expect to race in handicaps later on. It raises his handicap weight by just that much, and you cannot afford to give away weight unnecessarily.

I want to offer an idea that I have about lightweight and heavyweight jockeys. The old-timers preferred heavier boys, saying "I don't like to carry much dead weight." But for a great many years it has been my opinion that dead weight on a horse is much less harmful than live weight. Most of the dead weight used to bring lightweight riders up to the assigned impost is in the form of small, flat pieces of lead that are placed in a saddle pad made for that purpose. As much of the lead as possible should be in the front pockets of the pad. The pad should be placed as far forward as possible on a horse's withers, which to my mind is the strongest part of a horse. There it is buckled down under the saddle so it cannot move. It thus is carried on this very strong point in the horse's structure, and unlike live weight it cannot move forward or backward or shift from side to side.

If it could be tested I am sure it would be found that part of Eddie Arcaro's success is the result of his getting his weight well forward on his mount's withers. He crouches there as low as possible and sits as still as he can. But even so I don't think he can quite offset the weight differential between himself and a boy as light as Willie Shoemaker, who carries more lead in his saddle pad. I don't mean to compare the abilities of these two great riders. I am just using them as examples of light and heavy jockeys who were riding in good form at the time these notes were written. I can name innumerable instances of lesser saddle lights or even very inferior riders who were small in size and seemed to win more than their share of races. I think the lead their mounts carried on the withers as a result of their light weight accounted for their more frequent victories against heavier jockeys.

Shoemaker at work: Dead weight does not shift its position.
(Photo courtesy of Thoroughbred Publications, Inc.)

Arcaro at work: Forward, low, and still as possible.
(Photo courtesy of Thoroughbred Publications, Inc.)

I came to this conclusion about lightweight riders quite a long time ago, though during my early days as a trainer I never heard any comment on the matter except that horsemen always said they didn't like dead weight on their horses. For a number of years I thought that I was probably wrong about it and that I was alone in thinking that dead weight was better than live weight. But one day I read a note in an English paper, quoting a great English handicapper as agreeing with my belief, and saying that Tod Sloan was also of this opinion. I then felt better about my idea, and since then I have not doubted its soundness. Another consideration in favor of small boys is that they offer less wind resistance than bigger boys. Incidentally, it was Tod Sloan, a sensational jockey of his day, who introduced the forward crouching position in England. It was then called "monkey crouch."

Stable Management

A TRAINER learns through experience that there are a thousand little details of management which if properly carried out will help the performance of his horses. First he must pick a good assistant and then he must have a top foreman. It is the duty of these two to relieve a trainer of many of the little details of stable operation which would take up a lot of his time if he had less experienced assistance.

One of the most important aspects of stable management is the selection of feed. All feed must be inspected when it is brought into the stable. Bedding is nearly as important as the feed itself, because a horse may eat some of his bedding, especially if he is a good feeder. Therefore it is important to have good clean straw. Poor feed or bedding should be rejected. Food for horses, like food for people, must be of top quality. You cannot sacrifice quality in order to save a few dollars. In the long run there will be no saving because the poorer condition of your horses means less earnings in purse money. The weights on feed and bedding should be carefully checked. The feed dealer may be perfectly honest, and yet you can be shorted through carelessness or error on the part of a clerk.

Grooms and exercise boys must be carefully selected. They may be weeded out as you learn about their capabilities. Saddles, bridles, and other equipment must be first class and well cared for. They should be systematically inspected for wear or defects. A faulty bridle rein, girth buckle, or stirrup webbing may break and cause a bad accident. Blankets and coolers used on horses should be kept clean and in good repair. There should be rain sheets to protect horses going to and from the paddock in bad weather.

Each groom should be allotted equipment for which he is responsible: rubbing rags (very expensive these days), brushes, bandages, pins, scrapers, and other items. The equipment should be maintained in good condition, and each groom should have a box to keep it in. From time to time these boxes should be inspected to see that they are neatly kept and that the equipment is in good order. It should be required of every groom to keep his stalls clean and free from odors.

Each exercise boy is furnished a saddle and bridle, which he is expected to sponge and soap and keep in serviceable order.

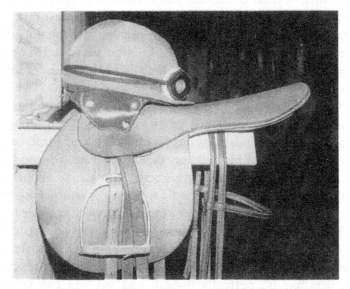

Each exercise boy is furnished a saddle and bridle, which he is expected to sponge and soap and keep in serviceable order. (Photo courtesy Suzie Oldham)

The stable foreman is in charge of all medicine, which he keeps in a closet and issues to the grooms when they need it. He and his first assistant (when there is an assistant; in the larger stables it is necessary to have several of them) check on the use of all medicine and leg paints.

The foreman selects the articles to be sent to the paddock with a horse that is to race. From experience he knows what is needed in the paddock and he is familiar with any special equipment that is required by a particular horse. An important item of paddock equipment is a small bottle of antiseptic to be used on cuts. An immediate application of antiseptic to cuts received by a horse during a race often prevents infection. The foreman must always be notified of any change in equipment on a horse so it will not be forgotten when he packs his tack before going to the paddock. The smallest detail forgotten can be very costly and possibly may cause one to lose a good race.

A shoeing record is kept in the stable so there is no possibility of letting a horse go too long without getting his feet manicured and putting new shoes on him. It is necessary to change the shoes on some horses about every two weeks. As a rule, three weeks is about right for most horses, but no horse should be allowed to go for more than four weeks without a change of shoes or a reset on his old ones. Each groom is held responsible for the condition of his horse. He is instructed to report immediately any slightest change about his horse. This applies to feet, legs, or in fact any part of the horse, and of course includes the shoes. He should tell the foreman when his horse needs the services of a plater. However, as there are good and bad grooms, and intelligent and unintelligent ones, as in every other business, the foreman and the assistant trainer must continually check all such things so no tiny detail is ever overlooked.

The trainer is responsible for the racing colors. Enough of them should be on hand so the jockey can wear a neat set of colors in every race. This is very important to an owner who takes pride in the stable and in the appearance of everything connected with it.

I could go on mentioning these little details almost indefinitely. There are hundreds of them, but these are the most important ones. The trainer is chiefly responsible for the smooth operation of a stable, but many of the less important details can be shifted to the foreman or assistant trainer. The trainer's time thus can be devoted to more important things.

It has been found beneficial to stable morale and teamwork if the grooms and exercise boys are given bonuses when a race is won by one of the horses. The custom is almost universal, although in some stables the employees have indicated that they would rather receive a little more in wages than to get a bonus. The bonuses in my particular stable are divided so all employees receive a little share in each winning purse, rather than paying bonuses only to the groom and exercise boy of the winner. Our men voted on this, and the majority favored the system we use. The result is that when a Brookmeade horse returns to the stable after a race, several men are ready to pitch in and help with him. The men and boys are interested in all the horses instead of just the three that are in their care.

The selection of a stable jockey is generally made by the stable owner, but usually with the advice of the trainer. When an outside jockey is required for a particular race it falls to the trainer to obtain the services of the best rider available. The trainer is in a better position to know which riders can be obtained, and he should know which jockey suits his horse under certain conditions.

The advantage of having a contract rider in the stable is that you have a boy who has the interest of the stable at heart, who knows all the horses, and who is always available. But there are some disadvantages. For one thing an owner invariably uses the contract jockey on every starter from the stable, even though now and then a few pounds could be saved by employing a lighter jockey. Again, a trainer might be able to obtain the services of a stronger rider or one better fitted to a particular horse in the stable whose peculiarities may make him difficult for the contract rider to handle.

One is nearly always obliged to use a contract rider. Sometimes they are a bit temperamental, and if you use another boy they think it is a reflection on their riding ability. This will eventually, if not immediately, lead to friction between the stable and the rider. I remember distinctly that John Rogers, one of my pet "greats" among the trainers of my early days, would often ride an outside jockey to save a few pounds of weight. This was when he was training for W. C. Whitney and had two excellent contract jockeys. It was said of Mr. Rogers that he would not let one of his horses carry a single pound of overweight if he could help it.

One of the most successful trainers of today has used more apprentice riders on his horses than any trainer I can remember. I refer to Hirsch Jacobs. I have never talked to him about his reasons for this, but I think it is mainly a question of getting a weight concession for his horses. Of course he doesn't use just any little apprentice who comes along, but picks one who is winning consistently and is at the top of his form. Because he always carries a large number of useful selling platers it is easy for him to obtain the services of popular young apprentices. Their agent-managers are quick to see that in riding for Mr. Jacobs they are continually getting good mounts for their "bug" boys and keeping them on the up-swing.

A boy under contract to an owner is considered an apprentice until he has ridden a prescribed number of winners or until he has ridden for a stipulated length of time after winning his first race. Then he becomes a full-fledged jockey, or as they say, a journeyman. Apprentices get an allowance of seven pounds until they have ridden 20 winners, after which they receive a five-pound allowance until a year after the date of their first winning race. Thereafter they receive three pounds when riding for their contract employer, provided he is the original maker of the contract. This rule is uniform throughout most of the United States. The apprentice allowance may be claimed in all claiming and allowance races but not in handicaps or stakes.

If I were pointing out the more important lessons for a trainer to learn I would impress upon him to think first of all of the general health and welfare of his horses. Their feed tubs should be watched religiously. If a horse doesn't clean up his feed it may mean that he is getting too much work or that he is being overfed or improperly fed. It could mean, too, that the feed is bad or of poor quality. Any of these things should be corrected immediately. If a horse doesn't eat a fair amount of hay, some attempt should be made to increase his appetite for it, because hay is his principal roughage. He will not hold a good barrel if he is not a good hay eater. Hay will be discussed further in the chapter on feeding. If a horse passes up a meal entirely, it is probable that he is sick. His temperature should be taken at once.

The temperature of each horse in the stable should be taken every morning, and the thermometer also should be used whenever a horse leaves his feed or doesn't act just right. The normal temperature of a horse may range from 99 1/2 degrees to 100, but a few fifths of a degree above or below this could be normal for some horses. Of course the temperature of a horse just coming out of a race or a work or from some other excitement can easily be a little above normal. The temperature of a young horse may flare up quickly, and it will go higher than for an older horse, but it may subside just as quickly after treatments. In addition to taking a horse's temperature every day as a routine checkup on his general welfare, it is also very important that his feet and legs be examined. If a slight swelling or fever is found and treated immediately, some very serious trouble may be avoided.

Horses that acquire bad stable habits such as stallwalking or weaving should get special attention in an effort to cure them of the habit, or at least minimize it. Such habits cause a horse to become listless and to race badly, because they take too much out of him.

It is very important that a horse have good manners. He should be schooled to break fast and straight from the starting gate. Most important, a horse should never be permitted to do so much in his workouts that he hasn't anything left for his race. This is the responsibility of the trainer. He should study a horse as an individual. While I contend that a horse will not race well if he is over-trained, a great amount of study is required to determine how much work is needed by an individual horse. Work that will knock out one horse may not be sufficient to fit another horse for a race. Needless to say, to win races a horse must be fit and not be trained past the point of fitness.

When a stallion or a mare is being permanently retired from racing and is to be sent to a breeding farm, it will be beneficial if they receive a short period of "unwinding" before they leave the track for the farm. A gradual let-up from the strenuous work of training and racing will enable them to adjust themselves to the quiet routine of a farm much more easily than if they are suddenly transplanted from the race track. The unwinding is accomplished through light training and short, easy works for a period of several weeks, if the time is available. Horses that are taken from the track to the farm without having a chance to become gradually adjusted to the change in tempo sometimes lose flesh and become quite nervous for a while.

A practice in our establishment, and a custom that is usually followed in other stables, is to divide the horses into three sets for their morning work-outs. A list is posted on the tackroom door, giving the names of the horses in the various sets, their exercise boys, and the work they are to do, whether they are to walk, gallop, or breeze. This avoids confusion in getting the horses ready. The makeup of the sets is worked out by the assistant trainer after he has received from the head trainer the names of the horses to be worked, and it is the assistant who, with the approval of the head trainer, selects the mounts for each exercise boy. Sometimes light boys are used on horses that are scheduled for a fast work. Some horses always require the best boys in the stable. Boys who are not so skilled or who are just beginning to learn must be given quiet mounts. Where one has a contract rider in the stable, he is used mostly on horses that have something fast to do. It is a very good idea to request an outside rider who has been engaged for a particular horse to come over in the morning and acquaint himself with the horse in a workout.

The posted list of horses lets each groom know which horses he must prepare. When a set of horses is ready, the foreman inspects them, and they are all brought out together. The trainer also gives the horses a quick inspection to see if there are any little changes he wants to make. If some slight detail has been overlooked, his experienced eye generally catches it. The exercise boys are given explicit instructions as to what to do with the horses.

After a gallop or a workout on the track, the horses are brought back to the stable and the preparation for their proper cooling out is begun. It is not advisable to have water or feed of any kind available to a horse following a hard workout. A horse is very easily foundered by too much water or feed at this time. He also can choke himself by grabbing a mouthful of feed when he is hot and excited. When a horse first comes in from the track, if it is a hot day, he gets a good bath and a rubdown with lukewarm water, to which has been added a body wash prepared for this purpose. Care must be taken in preparing this mixture not to have it too hot or too strong. The water should be about body temperature. Body washes usually contain alcohol and mild liniment, and something to tone up the hair.

Here I must say that I strongly disapprove of washing a horse on a cold day. If a trainer feels that a horse's muscles need a little stimulation on a cold day, I suggest rubbing in a little alcohol diluted with lukewarm water, about body temperature.

After a horse receives his washdown, he is covered with a blanket and is walked until he is thoroughly watered off and cooled out.

Three or four good swallows of water may be given to him every two or three rounds of the walking ring, or every time around if he is walking around a big stable. Most stables have a good outside ring where the horses are walked when the weather permits, but it is frequently necessary to cool the horses out under the shed because of inclement weather or a cold wind.

Cooling out after exercise. (Photo courtesy of Suzie Oldham)

The cooling-out process should always be under the direct supervision of the trainer or his assistant. It is one of the very important details of training. Sometimes a horse may cool out within 30 or 40 minutes after a slow gallop, but it is nearly always necessary to give them at least 45 or 50 minutes if they have had fast work. On hot and humid days it may take much longer. If a horse is put into his stall before he is properly cooled out, he can take cold easily or develop a soreness in his muscles.

On most days following a hard workout, a horse in racing condition is given only walking exercise, without a rider up. I make a point of having my horses walked at least one hour on these occasions. Experience has taught me that a horse requires this much exercise on his off days.

The procedure for cooling out a horse after a race is the same as when he has taken a serious workout. If a horse has been properly cooled out he can be fed any time after he is put away, if it is feeding time, but I don't like to feed a horse for at least 1 1/2 hours, or longer, after a hard race.

After a horse receives his washdown, he is covered with a blanket and is walked until he is thoroughly watered off and cooled out. (Photo courtesy of Suzie Oldham)

I always try to have at my stable a good sand bed in which the horses can roll every day that is fairly warm and sunny and the sand is dry. I have the boys let them roll after their work or after a race. They also enjoy grazing a bit before they are put away, if one has a little grass plot at the stable. Rolling in the sand and grazing help them cool out.

In arranging the sets of horses that are to be worked out, it must be taken into consideration that some horses are too rank to work with others, and of course one finds a horse now and then who will not work alone. Thought must be given to these details when the horses are selected for each set. If you have a horse that requires company all the way in his work, and you don't have another horse ready to go the full distance with him, it becomes necessary to work two horses with him. One will carry him for the first part of the work and the other will join in for the latter part. This is a difficult operation. It requires good exercise boys and careful timing on their part. Fortunately, it doesn't have to be done very often.

Horses enjoy rolling in the sand after cooling out. If they are put away before being properly cooled, they may take cold.
(*Photo courtesy of Suzie Oldham*)

The lighter the weight carried in a workout the longer the horse will last, provided you don't sacrifice experience in order to get a light boy. I like the light weight, but I would rather carry heavier weight on a horse than to risk an accident by using a light boy who lacks the necessary experience and ability.

A trainer is the judge as to when a horse requires blinkers, either in a race or in a workout. Blinkers should never be used in a race until the horse has worn them in several workouts. If blinkers are to be used on a horse in a race, and he has not carried them in his last previous race, permission must be obtained from the stewards before they can be used. The rules of racing require that a trainer obtain permission from the stewards before making any changes in the equipment used on a horse.

The use of blinkers is sometimes controversial, so perhaps a discussion of them would be appropriate at this point. Blinkers are used more frequently in America than anywhere else. They were first used on driving horses in the form of blinds or blinders. They were mainly put on horses that "saw too much" or shied from things they saw. They were also found to be helpful with laggards. A buggy horse usually wasn't too much afraid of a whip if he could see it. He knew when a crack was coming, but he was a different horse with blinders on, realizing that at any moment he might receive a crack of the whip and not have a chance to quicken his pace so the driver would only feint with the whip and not hit him.

Blinkers on running horses serve the same purpose. They keep a horse from swerving, because he doesn't want to swerve when he can't see what he might be swerving into. Horses wear many different kinds of blinkers, depending on what their trainers think they need. We have what are called the regular or closed blinkers. The use of blinkers began with this type. They permit a horse to see only straight ahead.

The French were among the first to use blinkers on steeplechase and hurdle horses. Someone over there had a set of blinkers made that extended out to the side but did not obscure so much of a horse's vision, with the idea that a horse needed to see a little more in jumping than on the flat. These blinkers were quickly adopted in America, being known as French or open blinkers. Later on, Ben Jones discovered that the use of a blinker with only one cup, and that on the right, or outside eye, leaving unobstructed vision in the left eye, would discourage a horse from bearing out. He can see the rail with his left eye and is discouraged from bearing to the right. This just about cured Whirlaway of his bad habit of bearing out, which probably had cost him several good races. Some trainers later went so far as to have the outside cup completely closed, so the horse's right eye was entirely covered. This was a satisfactory deterrent to bad runout horses and cured a great many of them. However, it was found that a horse running in a blind blinker frequently would bolt to one side or the other when in a bunch of horses and cause dangerous interference. The stewards in some localities therefore barred these blind blinkers except on horses with a blind eye. It is necessary to cover a blind eye because the eye is so sensitive that unless it is protected from flying objects the horse may injure himself, his rider, and other horses if struck in the blind eye by a clod or a stone.

Whirlaway and his one-cup blinker. (*Photo courtesy of NYRA*)

Some horses, having been taught to run close to the inside rail, develop a habit of bearing in, often causing interference in a race if they are not in an inside position. Frequently they run so close to the rail that their rider is afraid to let them run their best, for fear of an accident. I have found that by using a cup blinker on the inside eye, leaving the outside eye uncovered, such horses will not tend to bear into the rail so strongly.

It is not unusual to see a field of horses go to the post in England or on the continent without any blinkers, whereas it is not uncommon to see a field go to the post in America with every starter wearing blinkers. Some of this may be due to the difference between racing on grass and on dirt. Dirt, especially from a sandy track, gets in a horse's eyes, but they get very little dirt in their faces on the grass tracks abroad. Blinkers not only encourage a horse to do his best but they ward off some of the flying dirt.

The problem of cribbers is met by every trainer sooner or later. A cribber is a horse who takes hold of a board or other projection in his stall and sucks air through his mouth. The air is swallowed and goes into his stomach. Cribbing is a nervous habit that a horse may acquire by himself or pick up from another horse. In a stable where the horses are under close supervision at all times, cribbing may he detected at its very beginning. Often the animal can be cured if the necessary measures are taken early enough. There are special neck straps sold by harness dealers to prevent cribbing. They apply pressure at the throat and become uncomfortable when a horse swallows air. One of these straps should be put on a horse at the first sign of cribbing, and anything that a horse can grasp between his teeth while he is cribbing should be removed from his stall. His feed box should be left in the stall only long enough for him to eat, so he won't be tempted to crib on it. Sometimes it will be noticed that a horse is chewing on the boards at some particular place in his stall. This could lead to cribbing, so in all such cases the places where he has been chewing should be covered with something distasteful to him, such as tar, red pepper, or soap.

Any nervous habit is a bad habit with a race horse, but cribbing is worse than some of the others because a cribber draws a lot of air into his stomach, which affects his breathing when he races. There is another type of windsucker that is even worse than a cribber. This is the horse that raises his head, curls his upper lip, and just sucks wind without taking hold of anything with his teeth. Special bits are made to prevent such horses from sucking in too much air. They are round bits, like a short piece of pipe with a great many holes in it. They work on the principle that the air, when sucked in, swirls through the holes in all directions, so the horse cannot swallow as much of it as he would without the bit in his mouth. He cannot eat as well with such a bit in his mouth, and as a rule such a horse is likely to lose weight and condition more rapidly than a cribber. I would rather have two cribbers to contend with than one of these windsuckers, but fortunately we find them much less frequently.

Feeding

FEED is one of the most important items in a racing stable. Each purchase must be carefully inspected. Oats should be clean and weighty, with a good, meaty kernel. Whether or not they are clipped is unimportant, but they should have been well screened to get most of the dust out of them. Musty oats are easily distinguishable by their smell. A horse's nose is just as good as a man's, and he will not eat musty oats. If the oats are white, they should have a bright, clean color. However, there are very good gray oats and very good black oats. The good black oats are seldom seen in this country, but I have seen excellent ones raised in England. Crushed oats are very good when you can get them freshly crushed. They are especially good for gluttonous horses who swallow a good portion of their grain without chewing it. If you will examine the droppings of such a horse, you will find many whole oats that passed through undigested; the horse could not have gained any nourishment from them.

Yellow corn is the best corn for horses. It must, however, be of the first quality, and it must not be too hard. Some trainers feed cracked corn, but I personally prefer to feed it on the cob. Like oats, corn should be sweet to the taste and have no musty odor. If there are a few bad ends on the cobs, as one will nearly always find in corn, they must be removed from the ear before the corn is fed to a horse. Corn is a better winter feed, as it is supposed to be "heatening." However, a little of it can be fed all the time, because it puts flesh on an animal better than any other grain.

Some trainers throw one or two handfuls of barley or wheat into a horse's feed, especially when they feed mashes. Wheat sometimes will help a horse whose bowels are continually loose. I always try it in such cases, but I have had more success with wheat flour, browned in a pan on top of the stove. A handful of this in a horse's drinking water once or twice daily will help an ordinary case of scours. If this doesn't help, and soon, you may have a serious case for the veterinarian.

The cooked mashes which were always fed by the old-timers have about gone out of style. Here again I might mention John Rogers, trainer for W. C. Whitney, as he was the first man I can remember who stopped feeding cooked mashes. He said they were an unnatural food for a horse, as did Sam Hildreth, who stopped using them shortly afterward. Before that time, every stable had a big cooker for its mashes. Mashes were fed almost every night during the winter and frequently during the summer months. Mashes do put flesh on a horse, but I found that horses fed on cooked mashes were much softer physically than those not receiving mashes, and I stopped feeding them a great many years ago. Sometimes on a cold day or after a hard race I have my foreman pour boiling water over a good feed of oats and bran, with perhaps a handful of cracked corn in it, for the night feed. This is fed warm, but one must be careful not to give it to a horse when it is too hot. I sometimes feed a similar mash made with cold water, especially to a horse that is inclined to be a little constipated.

Raw linseed oil, or the raw meal, is a fine thing to add to the night feeding, especially in the winter or early spring. This must be carefully introduced into a horse's diet, however or he will leave his feed. It is best to mix a very small portion of it in the feed for a few days until the horses become accustomed to its taste. I have always endeavored to buy the raw linseed oil direct from the mill. In this way one is sure of getting good fresh oil, and it is far better than the meal. A good way to feed the oil is to mix it half and half with limewater, making an emulsion. A horse will take from half a teaspoonful to a cupful in his feed once a day.

An excellent powder to feed in late winter and early spring is made by mixing equal parts of cream of tartar, sulfur, and oil meal. A tablespoonful is fed at each meal, but this too must be gradually introduced into the feed because of its taste and odor. I recommend feeding this for about 15 days, then stopping for 15 days, then resuming for another 15 days, and so on. In this way it can be fed over a period of several months. A trainer will find that his horses will shed their winter hair earlier and will have nice, sleek coats much sooner than if they are not fed something like this.

Oats to a horse are like beefsteak to a man. A horse gets his strength and energy from grain. Most horses will eat only a certain amount of grain, but there are exceptions to this rule. Gluttonous horses will eat grain until they get beyond their capacity. What has always been considered a maximum quantity for a good feeder is 12 quarts a day of whole grain. This is sufficient for almost any horse in hard training when he is fit and ready to race. In fact, few horses will eat more than this. To my average normal feeders I give from 9 to 10 quarts of grain a day. A filly that eats 7 or 8 quarts a day is considered quite a good doer for a filly. There are plenty of little light fillies that get along very nicely on 6 quarts of whole grain a day. A quart of whole oats will make a considerably larger quantity when it is crushed.

The stable foreman generally does the feeding. It is up to him to find out just how much each horse requires. He tries to give them the amount they will clean up, not leaving any in the feed box, at each meal. The breakfast, or first meal of the day, is usually set out in the feed tubs at night, and the night watchman puts the feed tubs into the stalls between 3:00 and 4 a.m., so the horses will clean up their feed and have a chance to partly digest it before they are taken out for their morning work. The second meal of the day is fed about 11 a. m., and the last feeding comes at 5 o'clock. These hours may vary slightly in different stables.

The morning meal is always the smallest one, and the evening feed is the big one. If a horse eats nine quarts a day, he will be fed 2, 3, and 4 quarts at the morning, noon, and evening feeds, respectively. However, as I mentioned above, the foreman must acquaint himself with the eating habits of his horses so he will know how much to give each horse at every meal. The idea is to have the horse enjoy his meals, and yet not stuff him with so much grain that he will not eat enough hay, because hay is a very important item of his diet. It is hay that keeps a little flesh on a horse, and unless he is a good hay eater it is hard to race him and have him hold any flesh.

The man who does the feeding in a stable must know what he is doing, or else he must be watched and instructed continually. The trainer who does not keep himself informed as to how his horses are eating will wind up doing a very poor job. If a horse goes off his feed, his work must be lightened up. But if he eats everything that is given him and seems a little distressed after his works, then he is not getting quite enough work.

My favorite hay is a mixture of good quality timothy and clover, either alsike or red clover. A mixture of about 50-50 timothy and clover is very good. Sam Hildreth, who was tops in feeding, as he was in training, fed mostly on very heavy clover, while on the other hand my very good friend "Sunny Jim" Fitzsimmons has been known to feed straight timothy. In any case, a trainer should examine hay very carefully. I feel that it is essential for a horse to eat plenty of good hay. Hay furnishes the roughage that is so necessary to a horse.

Good hay will have a bright color and a sweet smell. Sometimes the outside of a bale will not look so good after it has been exposed to air, sunlight, and weather. When hay is delivered to a stable, a bale should be opened immediately. If the hay is dry and looks like a bunch of sticks, all brown in color, have the feed man take it away at once. The worst thing you can discover in hay is a musty odor. Never allow a flake of musty, moldy hay to be fed to one of your horses. I really believe that a great many horses have turned out to be roarers from having been fed moldy, bad hay, and there have been some deaths attributed to moldy hay. It does not take a man very long to learn how to tell good hay from bad, and it is as necessary for horses to have good hay as it is for them to have top-quality oats.

I feed very little alfalfa hay to my horses in training. To me it is a wonderful cattle feed and a good feed for broodmares and young horses, and it helps fatten a horse during the winter. But even during the winter months I have always fed alfalfa as I would eat a salad myself, throwing in a small handful not oftener than once a day. I have always felt that alfalfa is hard on a horse's kidneys when he is in heavy training. I believe that giving him all the alfalfa he could eat would be as harmful as throwing in a bushel of carrots. Two or three carrots are fine for a horse; horses enjoy carrots just as a man enjoys an apple. We generally cut them up and mix them with a horse's feed once a day. This helps the poorer feeders.

Horses love pea hay, but it is almost impossible to obtain pea hay that has been properly cured. It is a very heavy and fattening feed, but it molds easily and is difficult to cure. Now and then one can get a small quantity of pea hay that has not been rained on and has properly cured. It is then a beautiful green color, full of peas, and has luscious green leaves. Horses will leave any other feed I have ever seen for pea hay.

Most racing stables use some kind of green feed every day besides carrots. Usually they buy red clover, but at certain times of the year we get dandelion greens, which are very good for horses, and we even feed lettuce and cabbage occasionally. Horses like to pick grass for themselves, so no opportunity should be overlooked when one's horses can be held out on the grass to graze a bit. However, there is one little precaution that I suggest about feeding green stuff. Some horses should be allowed only a little green feed, or none at all, on the night before a good workout or a race. Green feed will make some horses blow to the point of distress, and several horses I have trained that bled slightly had too much green feed too close to a work or a race, in my opinion.

Horses should be drawn in their feed, that is, fed lightly, and this applies especially to those that are big feeders, before a hard workout or a race. If a trainer fears that a horse's last workout prior to a race was not quite sufficient, the error may be partly corrected by cutting the feed drastically. A horse is more likely to run a poor race on a full stomach, especially if he has been not too well prepared.

It is necessary always to have good fresh water in a horse's stall. His bucket should be emptied out and refilled with fresh water at least twice daily, and the watchman should be instructed to keep the water buckets full during the night. Of course a horse's bucket should be removed from the stall after his midday meal has been eaten if he is to race that afternoon.

As for his diet on race day, a horse gets his usual breakfast. It may be necessary to cut his midday meal considerably or give it earlier than usual if he is in one of the earlier races. There should be at least four hours, or a little more, between his second meal and the time of the race. On race day he is given only a handful of hay in the morning. In the case of big feeders it is often necessary to muzzle them after the midday meal, because they can fill up on straw if their hay is taken away. Particular care should be taken in drawing a horse that cribs. A little feed in his stomach, along with the air that he has swallowed, is very bad for a cribber.

If a horse has been given a sharp, short dash on the day before a race, an hour's walking on the morning of the race will be sufficient preparation for him.

Care of the Feet

SEVERAL KINDS OF SHOES are used at different stages of training. As mentioned before, I have found it a good plan to use tips, or half shoes, on yearlings. Then I go to full shoes, generally a medium-weight steel shoe with a blunt toe. As the horses progress in their training I may try steel shoes with sharp toes, but when racing I usually use aluminum shoes with sharp toes on all four feet, and a sticker on the outside of each hind shoe. If a horse goes down on his heels, I first try block heels on him, and if they don't prevent him from injuring his heels I try something else. Recently I have found that a jar caulk on one side and a sticker on the out-side of each hind shoe tends to work where block heels have failed. When nothing else seems to work I have used a trailer bar. These do the work all right, but I don't think a horse runs his best with them on.

On the sand tracks of today, it is absolutely necessary to find something that will protect a horse's heels, or you will run into a lot of trouble. Badly injured heels may keep a horse from racing for a long time. Generally we have to contend only with horses going down on their hind heels, but far too often we find horses that even go down on their front heels. It is usually not as hard to correct this as going down on the hind heels, but it is just as important that it be prevented.

Sometimes it is necessary to use bar shoes on a horse. They are used on feet that have been spread or that have been fractured in some way. Some trainers use them on horses with weak feet. It is also generally necessary to use a bar shoe to protect a quarter crack. A bar shoe is used as long as necessary to protect an injured foot, but a trainer usually removes a bar shoe before he races a horse, provided he thinks the injury has been cured. Some horses are successfully raced in bar shoes, but I would rather give the injury plenty of time to heal and remove the bars 10 days or two weeks before a race.

99

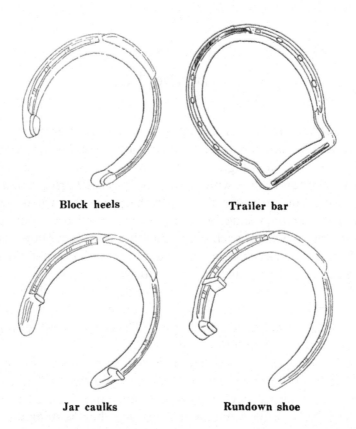

Block heels   **Trailer bar**

Jar caulks   **Rundown shoe**

Most horses are foaled with normal feet, and the majority of good farm managers will bring their yearlings to the market or to the racing stable with normal feet. This is easily done if proper care is taken right from the start. Young horses should have their feet leveled at intervals by a blacksmith, who sees that each foot has the proper frog pressure. This is accomplished by running a rasp across the bottom of the foot until the heels are level. When a horse's foot is level, both heels and the frog bear evenly on the ground. The leveling is done as often as necessary. The feet of young horses should never be allowed to go longer than three or four weeks without such attention. In the meantime, they should be watched closely, as there will be a difference in the rate of growth of the feet of various horses. In fact, it is not uncommon to find that the growth rate varies for each of a horse's feet. The left feet may grow faster than the right ones, or vice

100

versa. Hind feet are dressed in the same manner as the front feet, but it is not often that we have trouble with hind feet. Feet will grow much faster in wet weather than in dry weather, but it is dry weather that causes the most trouble. A horse's foot needs moisture. It dries up and contracts in hot, dry weather. When the weather is dry and the ground is hard, you have to look out for broken and ragged hooves.

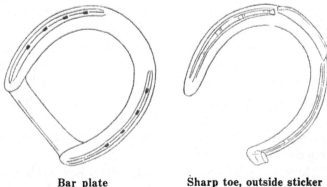

Bar plate   Sharp toe, outside sticker

If a man has a stream or a pool in his pasture that his young horses can walk in or stand in, he may avoid a lot of the trouble caused by heat and hard ground. The feet of young horses require careful attention. It is often necessary to put shoes on yearlings under these conditions to prevent their feet from being broken up too much.

Grooms in a racing stable should be required to keep their horses' feet clean at all times. It is easy to get thrush in a horse's feet if he is neglected for even a short time. Some trainers consider it a disgrace to find a case of thrush in their stable, but with all due care and attention it does happen once in awhile. There are a number of remedies for thrush. The oldest is butter of antimony. Bluestone is good. Creolin on a piece of cotton is about as good as anything. Thrush is not much trouble to cure if it is discovered in time. It can, however, go up into the foot and become chronic and even develop into canker.

A top blacksmith, who has learned his trade thoroughly and has had some years of experience, is invaluable to a racing stable. A careful man who really knows what he is doing will save a trainer a lot of heartaches. A great many injuries and breakdowns come from improper shoeing. It is only natural that a horse will strike and injure himself if his feet are not carefully leveled and his shoes put on properly. Some horses, because of their peculiar gait or some irregularity in the formation of their feet or legs, will invariably interfere and cut themselves when they are breezing. It takes a good man with plenty of experience to shoe such a horse so he won't injure himself.

Most horses are worked on by a good blacksmith, and as they grow older they quit cutting themselves, but now and then we come across one that is quite difficult. No corrective measures seem to work with him. With that kind of horse I always try giving him a good, long rest and then start him up again. To continue with a horse that is continually cutting himself is bad horsemanship. Such a horse, after having hurt himself, mixes up his gait worse than ever, in trying to protect himself. Boots and bandages are useful for protection against injury during morning workouts.

John E. Madden, who was very cranky about how his horses were shod, always had them stand on a level plank floor, and he religiously watched the blacksmith at work. He contended that if you stood the horse on a level floor you could tell when the foot was level. He would not permit a blacksmith to cut the frog, and in fact he hated to see a blacksmith use a knife on a horse's foot. He kept his horses' toes fairly short, the frogs level with the heels, and had the feet leveled with a rasp.

In any case of foot trouble, I think cold water or ice should be used to get the fever out, and then a mild irritant should be used around the coronary band to stimulate the growth of the foot. A lot of trouble can develop in the foot from dryness and fever. One of the oldest sayings on the race track is "No foot, no horse." This is true, because the foot is one of the most important parts of a horse's running machinery. For a great many years I have used Reducine around the coronary band and in the frog. It is hard to find anything better as a growth stimulant and counter-irritant. A very simple foot remedy is a mixture of 2 ounces of iodine and a pint of pine tar. Paint it on the bottom and the frog of a horse's feet once a day, as a stimulant and conditioner.

Minor Injuries

IN MY EARLY YEARS of training it was customary for a trainer to treat all slight illnesses himself, and take care of any minor injuries to his horses. It was a common thing to hear one of the younger trainers requesting help from a more experienced horseman regarding trouble in his stable, either sickness or injury. Veterinarians were few and far between. I guess at that time there was not enough veterinary practice to induce a good man to spend his life at such work.

Ed Corrigan, a well known character of the old days - he owned the Hawthorne race track and raced quite a stable of horses, even taking a fling at racing in England - once said that when a man hangs around the race track for a few years and gets so no-account that he can't make money enough to buy himself a square meal, and has the respect of nobody, everyone calls him "Doc." However, the race track veterinarians of today are very different men. We have veterinarians in all sections of the United States who are finely educated men and who have had years of experience. I might add that they are keeping up with the medicos who treat the human race, and are using many of the super-drugs that have been discovered in recent years. For this reason, and also because I am not qualified to write a veterinary medical treatise on diseases of horses, I am touching only lightly on a few of the things that a trainer might encounter on almost any of his training days.

The old training "greats," and my father was certainly one of them, seldom called in a veterinarian. They relied on their own vast experience, which of course they frequently had to do because first-class veterinary help was not often available. I was brought up in such a school, but like all the trainers of today I have learned to lean upon the veterinarian, for certainly he has greater knowledge and more experience in treating horses. After all, my business is training and his business is curing. Another present-day factor is that many horses are insured, and the insurance companies demand that a competent veterinarian be called in at once when a horse is sick or injured.

Now for just a few things that plague us regularly. I have already said that a horse's temperature is a pretty good indicator of his state of well being. If he has no fever, he isn't a very sick horse. Only today I had a horse refuse to eat or drink. Before I even saw the horse my foreman looked at him and thought his mouth was inflamed and sore. He swabbed it out with olive oil, and after a few hours the horse was okay. He guessed that the horse had in some way got hold of something that had blistered his mouth, we do not yet know what it was. It could have been an insect sting, but whatever it was, the foreman's judgment, based on his experience, did the trick.

I have had several accidents from using slow-feeding rings in my feed tubs. Fortunately they were slight, but when I heard of some other people's serious misfortunes because of these rings I immediately took them out of all my feed tubs. In case anyone doesn't know what these rings are, they are made of steel rods nearly as big around as one's little finger, and they are attached to the inside of the feed tubs, about halfway up from the bottom and about 1 1/2 inches from the sides. They are used to prevent a horse from throwing oats out of the tub, but he can get his lower jaw caught in the ring, and quite a few broken jaws have resulted. Some feed tubs have a little metal piece on the inside, like a shelf. These are quite satisfactory. These slow-feeding tubs prevent the wasting of feed and are also good for slowing down the gluttonous eaters who grab an enormous mouthful of grain and slobber it around.

When a stable is moving into a new location, the grooms should examine all the stalls carefully for anything that might injure a horse. Certain of the stalls may have been used for feed rooms, and have nails projecting from the walls, or nails may be sticking through from an adjoining stall.

Horses frequently pick up a nail in the foot. This is not too dangerous if taken care of immediately. It is necessary to give the horse a shot of tetanus antitoxin as soon as possible and cut the wound out to establish good drainage. If a horse steps on a nail that penetrates the foot deeply, the safest way to treat it is with a flaxseed poultice for several days, to draw out the soreness that is sure to result from such an injury. After a few days of poulticing it is safe to put a leather or aluminum pad on the horse and continue with his work. The pad protects the injured part in case the horse steps on a stone.

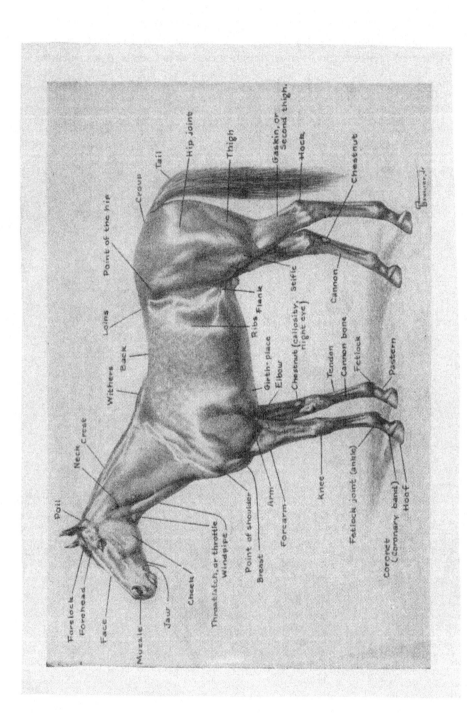

106

Miscellaneous Ailments

A HORSE'S TEETH can cause much trouble. I make a habit of calling in a specialist in horse dentistry when my yearlings have been accustomed to being handled sufficiently to permit the dentist to dress the teeth with a minimum of trouble. This first dressing should keep a horse's teeth in good shape for three or four months, when they should be looked at again. Five or six months after this they may need attention again, and they should be examined once more in the spring of the 3-year-old year. As a horse grows older his teeth don't require so much attention, but it is a good idea to have his mouth looked at from time to time to prevent trouble from developing. A horse's mouth is sensitive and is often hurt by the bit, anyway, so if his teeth are allowed to become sharp and cut his jaws, he may become altogether unmanageable. We have the mares at the farm checked over once a year.

Not as much trouble is encountered from periodic ophthalmia, or moon blindness, as in the old days. It has been discovered that with the proper use of riboflavin in the diet of a young horse, fewer cases of moon blindness are seen. The first sign of periodic ophthalmia is an apparent weakness of the eyes and a constant flow of tears from the corner of the eye. A trainer should call his veterinarian immediately upon noting such symptoms.

Horses have hives, just as people do, only the bumps are generally larger. A horse can become covered with them in just a few minutes. This is another illness that can be better left to the veterinarian than to home remedies, though I have never known hives to be dangerous or fatal.

Most fat yearlings will chafe where the saddle girth pinches them at breaking time. If the chafing is only slight, strong salt water will toughen the skin quickly enough so you won't lose much time with the horse. Salt is also a good remedy for cuts in the mouth, which occur so frequently.

A bad thing to fool with is a sore back, especially around the withers. Fistulas develop quickly on the withers, and they are very serious, so one must always be careful to have enough padding on the saddle, especially at the withers. We are likely to use our oldest saddles on yearlings, and when a saddle gets old the padding sometimes gets thin, and often a steel saddle tree spreads enough to allow it to press on the point of the withers. This frequently occurs with high-withered horses. My advice to young horsemen is to heed the first sign of soreness in this area and stop using the saddle until all soreness and inflammation have subsided.

We have a great many horses today with bad knees. The first sign of knee trouble is when a horse walks wide, spreading his front legs apart after a race or a workout. Slight fever may be noticed in one or both knees, and as the trouble progresses there will be swelling, generally on the front of the knees. The worse the condition becomes, the more fever and swelling will be present. Sometimes you can get by for a while with a young horse with bad knees by treating him with some sort of paint or other medication, but usually the condition becomes so aggravated that the horse must be given a rest. Most veterinarians have their favorite methods of treating bad knees, but it requires from three to six months, at least, to get good results.

One of the commonest and most serious injuries is a bowed tendon, almost always in a front leg. A bowed tendon is a rupture of the sheath which covers the rear tendon in a horse's leg, called the flexor tendon. The injury can come from a strain or it can be caused by a blow. Frequently it may result from a bandage that has been applied too tightly. It often occurs when a great strain is placed on the leg in a race or a workout. Many more cures are made with young horses than in those three years old and upward. Older horses always seem to break down again just when you think you have them ready to race. It often occurs in the last work preparatory to a race. To me it is never good policy to attempt to train a horse who has been bowed unless he has been given a solid 12 months rest. The great little steeplechase horse Battleship bowed when he won the Grand National Steeplechase Handicap in America. I had the pleasure and satisfaction of assisting in an advisory capacity in the eventual rehabilitation of this horse. Mrs. Marion du Pont Scott, his owner, gave him a full year's rest before putting a saddle on him again, and it was two years or more afterward that this great little horse won the coveted Grand National Steeplechase in England.

Another great horse that came to top form after having been laid up with a bowed tendon was Old Rosebud. It is results such as these that keep us hopeful and trying for a cure when one of our good horses breaks down. I am afraid, however, that cures are the exception, and for every horse that is brought back to winning form after having bowed a tendon there are 20 (or shall we say 50?) that disappoint us.

There are many and varied treatments prescribed by veterinarians or used by old-timers on bowed tendons. To my mind, the best treatment of all is to have the firing iron applied after the horse has had sufficient rest to allow the swelling and fever to subside completely. Then put on quite a severe blister over the firing, and follow this with one or two more blisters, each time allowing the scurf to drop completely off before applying another blister. Be sure that in all cases the horse gets his full 12 months rest, by which time the leg should feel hard and calloused and should carry no fever or swelling.

Splints are another common ailment which almost invariably require firing. (One newspaperman who wrote about Bold after he won the Preakness said we had to put splints on him and lay him up for a while.) Splints are bony growths which usually develop on the inside of the front cannon bone. Curbs, which are swellings on the rear of the hind cannon, used to be fired in the old days, but I think that frequently they are just lightly blistered nowadays. As a rule, curbs don't cause much trouble. Splints and curbs develop from a blow or a strain or a jar; neither splints nor curbs set a horse back in his training for very long. Equipoise was fired for splints as a 2-year-old at Saratoga and was back in training within two weeks or less.

The ailment that occurs most frequently in the region of the hock is a bog spavin. It usually occurs only in one hock, and the area may become greatly enlarged. It is advisable to rest a horse as long as he is lame from a boggy hock, but this is one ailment that usually subsides when a horse is kept in light work. My experience has been that a mild astringent paint or liniment is much more effective than strong medication. A bog is a large, soft swelling involving the front and sides of the hock. The first time Colin started, at Belmont Park in a race for maiden 2-year-olds, he came out with a great reputation and was the short-priced favorite. I was amazed when I looked at him in the paddock and saw that one of his hocks was almost twice the normal size. The swelling subsided to some degree later in his career, but the bog never interfered with his racing or training, as he was unbeaten in 15 races.

Now and then a horse will kick the walls of his stall or otherwise injure the back of his hocks, and develop what are called capped hocks. He generally will carry this blemish for the rest of his life, but it won't interfere with his racing. Both hocks on my good mare Tambour were slightly capped. A great many horses in Europe have capped hocks caused by bumping their hocks against brick stable walls, as nearly all the stables in Europe are built of brick.

We have a great deal of stifle trouble today. To me it seems much more prevalent than it was some years ago. Seemingly for no reason at all, a horse will begin to throw his stifle out of place and drag his leg. Generally, this is not too serious. It can be corrected to a considerable degree by putting block heels on the horse's hind shoes and using a tightener or blister on the point of the stifle. I have had excellent results from using Kincade's Anodyne. The stifle slippage seems to come from a weakness of the muscle that holds it in place. Horses afflicted in this way generally go along all right in their work, but they may have a recurrence if they have a rest period, so it seems best to keep them in work.

A good deal of trouble is encountered in present-day racing from broken sesamoid bones or the tearing of the ligaments attached to the sesamoids. A horse has two of these small, gristly bones at the rear of each ankle. They form a smooth surface to which certain ligaments are attached, and certain tendons slide over them. Due to the severe strain of running at high speed, these sesamoid bones are often actually pulled in two, or small pieces of them are torn off by the attached ligaments. They can also be broken by a blow from a horse's foot. If a sesamoid fracture is a simple break, it will heal in time, but I do not know of a case where a horse has raced well or has lasted very long after such a fracture has healed.

We also have split pasterns, which seems to be quite a common occurrence in England. This too, I think, is caused by a horse landing on a hard surface. They tell me that the turf in England gets quite hard during the dry summer months, so much so that owners refrain from running their best horses during that time. I have seen a few cases of split pastern. In most instances the horse's foot was so badly skewed to one side or another that no attempt was made to race them afterward. John Sanford's good horse Mohawk II who seemed to be the top 2-year-old of his year, winning all of his starts at Saratoga including the Hopeful Stakes under 130 pounds, split a pastern and his racing career was consequently shortened.

When a horse is seriously lame from a foot or leg injury it is always advisable to have X-ray photographs made to determine if there is a fracture. When a bone is fractured it requires considerable time to effect a cure, if a cure is possible.

All stables today equip their medicine cabinets with remedies for the little things that occur. They have colic medicine, given at the first sign of colic, and wound lotions. The lotions are always kept handy for treating slight injuries. Most people have their favorite fever medicines and diuretics, lots of different leg paints, liniments, blisters, and so on. If a trainer can diagnose a horse's trouble at once he administers whatever remedy he has at hand and calls the veterinarian. I could write for days about the many little things that cause grief for a trainer, but I'm sure that after I had described every ailment that I ever saw or heard of I would discover a new one in my stable the very next day. One soon learns that horses are fragile. Their mechanisms are approximately the same as humans, who are always developing a new ache or pain that the medicos have to find a name for.

Most stables use cotton and bandages on a horse standing in the stable. They are generally used after a leg has been treated with some kind of paint or lotion. A great many stables use cotton and bandages on a horse that is being taken to the paddock or when he is being shipped, and again a lot of horses are galloped in bandages with one or two sheets of cotton underneath. The use of bandages is controversial. Some people think they do more harm than good. Others use them only on horses that they think need some extra

111

protection. Some people use them all the time. Others don't think they are necessary at all. To me, this is entirely up to the trainer. He must learn for himself if and when to use bandages. The veterinarian will tell you when to use bandages in the treatment of a horse.

Racing Strategy

THE MISTAKE most frequently made by trainers is overmatching a horse. Sometimes they are persuaded to put a horse in a race because there are only a few entries. Now and then they win such a race, which tends to make them take such chances more often, but they cannot help but be badly beaten many more times than they win.

Another very common mistake is to hurry a horse to get him ready for a particular race whose conditions seem to fit him, instead of waiting for a similar race and giving him the necessary time to get into top racing condition.

It is a mistake to run a horse in the mud after he has shown a positive dislike for it. It discourages him. Some horses cut themselves badly every time they race in the mud, and even when they work in the mud in the morning. Yet some trainers think that it is absolutely necessary to give a horse a certain work on a particular day, even if the track is muddy. Like all trainers, I have made this mistake much more often than I should have, and the greatest percentage of the time it has been to my regret. However, I have learned this lesson quite well, now, and I work my horse as little as possible on muddy tracks, except of course in the case of horses that like the mud.

Often a trainer, especially one with little experience, will copy the training of another horse if he happens to have a horse preparing for the same race. As I have tried to bring out, no two horses are alike, and what is good fitting work for one may tear another horse all to pieces.

Just because you see a trainer send his horse a mile in 1:40 in a work, for example, is no reason why you should bring your horse out, if he is preparing for the same race, to see if he can work a mile in 1:39. There is every likelihood that the horses are dissimilar. A trainer must know and train his own horse, and disregard another's training.

I distinctly remember seeing Colin and Uncle in their preparatory work on the same day for the Saratoga Special. Uncle went six furlongs alone in 1:12 and a fraction, with his trainer slowing him down. A few minutes later Colin was worked with blinkers and a companion; he was ridden out six furlongs in 1:15. In the Special, which was run a few days later, Uncle went head-and-head with Colin for about three furlongs, after which Colin won very easily, running the six furlongs in 1:12. They were the only starters in the race. One was a free work horse and the other was a sluggish worker.

Had the trainer of Colin been a green man and not known his horse, he might have been frightened out of even starting his horse in the Special. As it was, everyone else was frightened out of racing against those two horses, and Colin, who had benefitted from exactly the sort of workout he needed, was the winner.

A great many mistakes are made in selecting jockeys, but often the trainer has to do the best he can with whatever jockey is available. Most jockeys are tied up by their contract stable, and in addition there is the matter of weight. You might like to ride a certain boy on your horse, but because of the weight you have to take a lighter jockey. The selection of a jockey, like the selection of a race to run a horse in, is pretty much left to the trainer by the owner. The trainer has to be smart enough to pick a good spot for his horse and then get ahead of the other fellow in engaging the best jockey available at the weight. As a rule, if you have a good jockey on your horse he requires very few instructions. With a boy in Eddie Arcaro's class, for instance, you generally give him a leg up and say: "Well, Eddie, he's all yours. Do the best you can." (I always have the utmost confidence in Arcaro. As he himself puts it, "I Ride to Win.")

However, there are many times when you use a jockey who has never ridden a particular horse, and you must be very careful to inform him of any peculiarities the horse may have when racing. Believe me, some of them have some tricks! One horse may like to race along the inner rail, while another will not run on the inside and must be brought around other horses. There are horses that bear in, especially at the finish of a race. Others bear out on the turn, or at the point of the turn, or only in the stretch. Some horses do not like to be tiptoed away from the barrier. Others won't run unless the boy

114

gives them a crack or two with the whip right at the start. Some like to run in front, others never win if they are taken to the front too soon. Some horses pull themselves up when taken between other horses. All of these things, and many more, should be known to the trainer, and unless a boy is cautioned beforehand, he may be caught napping and lose a race that he should win.

At times a trainer can analyze a race beforehand, and noting that his horse is the only one with speed, he may instruct his boy to take a slight lead and make the pace as slow as he can for as long as he can. This was the strategy used by Trainer John Gaver, of the Greentree Stable, in his instructions to Ted Atkinson on one occasion. Atkinson carried them out as no one else could have, and beat Ponder with Capot in the 1949 Belmont Stakes. Ponder was eating him up at the finish, but his move came too late; Atkinson had nursed his horse across the finish line. This was about as pretty a ride as I ever saw.

Sometimes, in looking over a race, a trainer may see a chance to lay off what should be a pretty fast pace. He may see two or more very speedy horses that most likely will be fighting for the lead. He therefore may instruct his rider to wait until the speedy ones have cut each other's throats. A smart rider will bring his horse through the stretch with a rush that will carry him past the tired pacemakers.

Sometimes a man is fortunate enough to have two pretty fair horses eligible for one of the good races. He may sacrifice the faster one to kill off the pacemakers, while holding the other horse for a late rush to the finish line. When running two horses under these conditions, a trainer should remember to caution his riders not to get in each other's way, and under no conditions to interfere with another horse in the race, because if one horse in an entry causes interference, both horses are subject to disqualification. There are very few disqualifications today because of willful fouling. Present-day jockeys are taught to ride fairly and to respect the other fellow's rights in a race.

If a man is starting two horses in a race in New York - and perhaps the rule applies in some other states - he is permitted to declare to win with one of the horses. He might want to do this if one horse has already been penalized in the weights because of previous victories, and he wants to keep penalties off the other horse. Or, if an owner or trainer has an unbeaten horse, he may want to extend his list of victories and declare to win with that horse.

Capot's victory in the 1949 Belmont Stakes:
"about as pretty a ride as ever I saw." (Photo courtesy of Bob Coglianese)

Declaring to win means that in case two horses of an entry come down in front of the field, the declared horse may go on and win and the other horse can be restrained behind him, provided of course that they have the rest of the field beaten. One of the classic happenings of this kind was when John Rogers, trainer for H. C. Duryea, raced the great filly Artful twice behind a stablemate. He thereby kept Artful's maiden allowance for the Futurity Stakes, which she won very easily, beating Tradition and the great Sysonby.

Owner-Trainer Relationships

IN ADDITION to worrying about his horse, a trainer must know how to get along with the owner or owners for whom he trains. After long experience he will learn that the owners are like the horses - they are all individuals and must be studied so there will be perfect understanding by both parties. I have heard it expressed that the relationship between an owner and his trainer is almost like that of a marriage, where both individuals must learn to give and take. The trainer must understand that the owner puts up the money and expects to get some pleasure in return, without being annoyed by every little irritating thing that comes up in the stable. These details fall upon the trainer, and it is up to him to solve his troubles without running to the owner, who probably is annoyed enough by the enormous bills he receives and the terrific jolts he gets through bad breaks. A great many of the tribulations come from blunders on someone's part, maybe the jockey, for whose actions the trainer is responsible because he chose him. Or possibly the trainer himself picked the wrong race, or maybe the stable is just having bad luck.

Great thought should always be given to operating the stable for the pleasure of the owner. Of course in this partnership the owner also has his responsibilities toward creating a harmonious atmosphere.

A conscientious trainer takes his losses with great concern. When he is beaten he is low in spirit, and the greater his fault in the matter the worse he feels. This is no time for an owner to jump on him with both feet. It is then that the owner should show himself to be a good sport, and a good sport is known by the manner in which he can take defeat.

A trainer is hired because the owner thinks he is competent and can do a good job, so the owner should not flare up at the first little thing that goes wrong. In racing there seem to be at least 20 disappointments for every happy landing. The sooner one learns to take these things philosophically, just so soon will he discover the great pleasures in racing.

Some trainers work on a salary for one owner. They are called private trainers. Others take horses in a per diem basis. They are called public trainers and they often have several owners, sometimes as many as a dozen where no one owner has many horses. Salaried trainers are paid so much a month and are reimbursed for their traveling expenses and any money which they actually pay out on behalf of the owner of the stable. Public trainers get so much per day for each horse trained by them. At present, the rate in localities where the price of feed and labor is high runs to about $12 a day. The usual extras for which an owner is billed by a public trainer include veterinary charges, shoeing, drugs, express or vanning expenses, and so on. Most owners furnish their own tack and such articles as blankets, blinkers, etc. in their own colors. A trainer further gets a percentage of a horse's winnings. This is usually 10 per cent, and covers second, third, and fourth monies as well as first money. He also gets a percentage on any horse sales he makes for an owner.

There is an old saying that no two men can train one horse. The conclusion to be drawn from this makes me say that an owner should hire a trainer in whose ability and integrity he has the utmost confidence, and then he should let him train the horses with very little interference, or preferably no interference at all. There have been in the past, and there are today, instances of perfect relationships between owner and trainer. They just seem to go on forever, as happy marriages do. I have to admit, however, that for every instance of this kind in America there are ten like it in most foreign countries, especially in England, where training jobs have been handed down from father to son for generations. When an owner and a trainer reach a point of perfect understanding and confidence in each other, it is then that both get the utmost in pleasure and success.

CLASS IN HORSES

I have often heard discussions about "class" in race horses. The question is asked: "Can you define class in a race horse?" There doesn't seem to be a concise definition of class, or at least I haven't found it. A horse has class, or he hasn't got it.

Great horses seem to develop class, but the fact is that they have had it all the time, but for various reasons it seems to come out late in some horses.

Some people think that class lies within a horse's head-that it is his will to win. This is certainly one of the greatest attributes a horse can have. One of the factors contributing to class seems to be the heart. It is known that the heart of the great horse Sysonby, whose skeleton is in the Museum of Natural History in New York, was half again as large as that of the average horse of his size. Sysonby had as much class as any horse I ever saw. His trainer, James Rowe, one of the greatest of all time, loved him as he would a human being, and wept like a baby when he died. We don't know where a horse gets his class, but we do know that a horse who has it needs to run only a few hundred yards head-and-head with a horse that hasn't got it, and the latter will pull himself up like a man putting the brakes on his automobile.

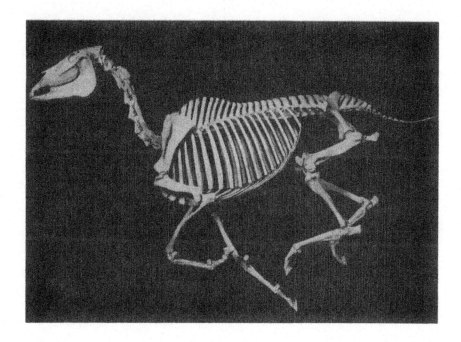

INDEX

We hope you enjoyed this title
from Echo Point Books & Media

Training Soccer Champions

Anson Dorrance with Tim Nash

Field strategy, motivational techniques, team dynamics, and much more are discussed in this must-have guide to coaching. With countless championship titles and numerous awards, Anson Dorrance knows what it takes to win, and now you can too.

Million Dollar Blackjack

Ken Uston

Contrary to popular opinion, anyone who enters a casino can win at blackjack. World famous blackjack expert Ken Uston provides seven simple rules to improve your game and presents students with four levels of winning skills.

Small-Scale Pig Raising

Dirk van Loon

Do you dream of raising a feeder animal but have limited land, time, and money? Covering everything from buying your pig to smoking your own bacon, van Loon explains how to produce the most meat for the smallest investment of time and money.

Mastering Pac-Man

Ken Uston

In this fully illustrated and comprehensive guide, master gamer Ken Uston reveals his secrets to this timeless game. Learn the strategies behind the game's main patterns and secrets to becoming a true Pac-Master.

Golf Fundamentals

Seymour Dunn

In this historic manual, discover the formula for optimal golf techniques that made Seymour Dunn a legend and will make you a master of the game.

Paul Runyans Book for Senior Golfers

Paul Runyan

In this book, the two-time World Senior Champion guides golfers over 50 how to play better, score better, and get more enjoyment out of the game. No one is more qualified to instruct senior golfers than Paul Runyan.

CPSIA information can be obtained
at www.ICGtesting.com
Printed in the USA
BVOW09s1211220118
505962BV00008B/158/P